WordS

Also available from ASQ Quality Press:

Managing with Conscience for Competitive Advantage
Pete Geissler

*The Certified Manager of Quality/Organizational Excellence
Handbook: Third Edition*
Russell T. Westcott, editor

*Effective Writing for the Quality Professional: Creating Useful Letters,
Reports, and Procedures*
Jane Campanizzi

*Everyday Excellence: Creating a Better Workplace through Attitude,
Action, and Appreciation*
Clive Shearer

*Making Change Work: Practical Tools for Overcoming Human
Resistance to Change*
Brien Palmer

*Leadership For Results: Removing Barriers to Success for People,
Projects, and Processes*
Tom Barker

*Inside Knowledge: Rediscovering the Source of Performance
Improvement*
David Fearon & Steven A. Cavaleri

Root Cause Analysis: Simplified Tools and Techniques, Second Edition
Bjørn Andersen and Tom Fagerhaug

The Quality Toolbox, Second Edition
Nancy R. Tague

SPC for Right-Brain Thinkers: Process Control for Non-Statisticians
Lon Roberts

To request a complimentary catalog of ASQ Quality Press publications,
call 800-248-1946, or visit our Web site at http://qualitypress.asq.org.

WordSuccess

Why and How to Express Yourself to the Good Life

Pete Geissler

ASQ Quality Press
Milwaukee, Wisconsin

American Society for Quality, Quality Press, Milwaukee 53203
© 2006 by American Society for Quality
All rights reserved. Published 2006
Printed in the United States of America
12 11 10 09 08 07 06   5 4 3 2 1

Library of Congress Cataloging-in-Publication Data

Geissler, Pete, 1933–
    WordSuccess : why and how to express yourself to the good life / Pete Geissler.
        p. cm.
    ISBN-13: 978-0-87389-699-3 (pbk. : alk. paper)
    1. Business communication.   I. Title.   II. Title: Word success.

    HF5718.G42   2006
    650.1'3—dc22

                                                                2006021175

Publisher: William A. Tony
Acquisitions Editor: Annemieke Hytinen
Project Editor: Paul O'Mara
Production Administrator: Randall Benson

ASQ Mission: The American Society for Quality advances individual, organizational, and community excellence worldwide through learning, quality improvement, and knowledge exchange.

Attention Bookstores, Wholesalers, Schools, and Corporations: ASQ Quality Press books, videotapes, audiotapes, and software are available at quantity discounts with bulk purchases for business, educational, or instructional use. For information, please contact ASQ Quality Press at 800-248-1946, or write to ASQ Quality Press, P.O. Box 3005, Milwaukee, WI 53201-3005.

To place orders or to request a free copy of the ASQ Quality Press Publications Catalog, including ASQ membership information, call 800-248-1946. Visit our Web site at www.asq.org or http://qualitypress.asq.org.

Quality Press
600 N. Plankinton Avenue
Milwaukee, Wisconsin 53203
Call toll free 800-248-1946
Fax 414-272-1734
www.asq.org
http://qualitypress.asq.org
http://standardsgroup.asq.org
E-mail: authors@asq.org

AMERICAN SOCIETY
FOR QUALITY™

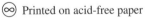 Printed on acid-free paper

Contents

PART III
Let's Talk Money, Big Money!   79

Preface

I wrote this book for all of you who want to be more successful in any or all parts of your lives, who want to understand more fully the precise connections between your skills with the language and being fulfilled, and who are willing to practice the simple habits of CLOWT (compartmentalize, listen, organize, write, test) and the Elite Eleven Tools, which make it all possible.

The book will appeal to managers who want their organizations to be more competitive, teachers at high school and college levels who want their students to get higher grades and a leg up on life, communications consultants who want to add credibility to their convictions that understanding each other is critical to our very being and functioning, government officials who are concerned with education, and anyone who wants to add understanding and empathy to his or her relationships of all types.

Many thanks to Tim Fitzgerald of the Johnson O'Connor Research Foundation, who provided me the full reports of its studies and verified the accuracy of my conclusions. Thanks also to the managers who agreed to be profiled simply because they subscribe fully to the premise: John Yasinsky, Jim Browne, Sherry Davis Guth, Joe D (who prefers to be anonymous), and Georgia Berner. My fondest hope is that you will extract enough meaning and inspiration from their experiences to emulate them.

I would be boorishly impolite not to thank Annemieke Hytinen, former acquisitions editor at Quality Press, who somehow saw the germs of a useful book in its premise and initial rough drafts, and Paul O'Mara, project editor, who demonstrated remarkable persistence and patience by reading and rereading subsequent drafts and suggesting improvements.

PART I
THE PRINCIPLES

Thirty minutes to motivation, inspiration, and behaviors that work.

1 The Launching Pad

The clear sequence from vocabulary to success, no matter how success is defined.

W̲e all want to be wealthier and happier; it's the global way. We all can be, simply by understanding and living the **SuccessAgon**:

The SuccessAgon.

I started developing the **SuccessAgon** a number of years ago when I ran across a decades-long study that links vocabulary to success in business so tightly that I was startled. I also felt that the leap from vocabulary to success was too big to be credible; surely some intermediate steps were missing.

They were, and they're expressed briefly in the **SuccessAgon** and more fully in this book. In essence, a larger vocabulary is the launching pad for success; it allows its possessor to clearly connect ideas, better understand the situation, make better decisions, communicate to others more precisely and persuasively, and be more successful. Those of you who own a bigger and better vocabulary think more clearly and logically, and you are less likely to be plagued by the bad decisions that can derail careers and lives. I have labeled you the "Articulates."

Uncovering the missing steps led to another unexpected and delightful discovery: success is far more than success in business and far more than promotions and money. Applying the **SuccessAgon** can translate quite nicely to the happiness that comes from an enriched and fulfilled life; the Articulates profiled in this book are successful businesspersons as well as successful human beings.

More recently I asked myself, if words can enrich our individual lives, why can't they do the same for families, communities, organizations, even countries? The answer, of course, is that they can. Any group can enjoy the significant advantages of a larger vocabulary, clearer connections of ideas, better decisions, and lucid communications.

If that seems like another leap of faith, I recommend that you examine the profiles of practicing Articulates in Part II. John Yasinsky, as detailed in Chapter 4, turned around a huge but shrinking company by first making sure that each employee, from his staff to the plant workers, understood his or her mission and expectations. Joe D, whose story appears in Chapter 8, breathed new life into an ailing division of a large company by insisting—some would say too forcefully—on clear, concise communications that satisfied customers without alienating them. Georgia Berner, as described in Chapter 9, put the need to be articulate in her company's mission statement and placed the statement in every plant and office. You'll find many similar examples throughout the book.

I found the many statistical, anecdotal, and historical incentives for being an Articulate to be powerfully compelling. You'll find the statistical incentives in Part I, the anecdotal incentives in Part II, and the historical incentives throughout.

Enjoy. Experience. Succeed.

2 What's in It for You

Just your career, income, relationships, and lifestyle.

"**K**nowledge is power."

This simple and short aphorism is so universally accepted that it's embedded in our everyday thinking and speech.

But it's only half right.[1] In fact, it's a dangerous half-truth and surely an exaggeration.

Here's why: knowledge without the ability to express it is a toothless, useless, sleeping tiger; knowledge by itself is powerless. The same is true for creativity, innovation, inventiveness, and other desirable and valued cerebral characteristics of humans.

"It is a luxury to be understood."

Ralph Waldo Emerson

Astute managers of every stripe, persuasion, and level—and others in any walk of life—know that being understood is a luxury beyond price; it is a fundamental necessity for their social and financial success, and for the viability of their organizations. They share one trait: all live the **SuccessAgon**; all are articulate. Together, they are the Articulates.

Articulate denotes that rare ability to express ideas, thoughts, policies, directives, and so on coherently, clearly, distinctly, and succinctly. Readers and listeners know the purposes of the communiqués and how to react. They are not misled.

"Articulate" also encompasses those rare and inseparable abilities to compartmentalize, listen, and understand as prerequisites to expression. Some pundits would say that these abilities are the rarest of all talents in business and, in truth, in all human interactions. You can read more about them and the input/output nature of articulation in Chapter 3.

Note: My intent in this book is to confine "articulate" to expression and thinking via words, both spoken and written—the media used most often in business and other human endeavors. I do not deny that "articulate" applies to other media such as sculptures, paintings, music, and even body language, as pantomimists the world over demonstrate so eloquently. We can all agree, for example, that Mozart expressed his ideas, thoughts, and feelings with sublime articulation through his music, Picasso expressed his with an equal sublimity through his paintings, Homer through his poetry, and Chaplin with his rubbery face and dramatic gestures. I could cite countless other examples, as could you.

Colleagues with whom I tested the title and premise of this book found it difficult to agree with them, but perhaps their cynicism interfered. All scoffed at the preposterous idea of "articulate" in our society, including business. They are colored by the appalling, ear-screeching, mind-bending lack of articulation we are bombarded with every time we turn on the TV or open a newspaper, and they point to egregious errors in grammar and thinking in advertisements, articles, interviews, and just plain conversation.

They're right, of course, but only up to a point. Managers already at or near the top or on the rise are a different breed; they can decry the slaughter of English in the popular media (and even in their organizations) and not become part of the problem, and *not promote people who are.*

The bottom line is that articulation is still revered and rewarded in business, government, and other organizations, as the people you'll meet later in this book demonstrate clearly. They'll explain how being articulate was not the only, but certainly a key driver in their rise up the organization's ladder and an important reason for their satisfaction with their personal lives—that elusive and desirable feeling called happiness.

Careful readers will ask at this point, why, if these managers are so wonderfully articulate, do they retain a writer to prepare their speeches and so on? One reason: most managers are articulate speakers; however, only a few are articulate writers as well. They struggle (a euphemism for investing an inordinate amount of time and sweat) with the mechanics of writing. Whereas they are absolutely certain of the main points they want to convey, they tend to be unsure of grammar, syntax, semantics, and tone, and they prefer to let someone else fight those hard-won battles. They also know that their time is better spent at what they do best—managing—and part of management is delegating to specialists who can complete certain tasks more quickly and inexpensively than they can.

> *"A mighty thing is eloquence ... nothing*
> *so much rules the world."*
>
> Pope Pius II (1405–1464)

Communication in any organization has been defined as the glue that holds the organization (or organizations) together or, for that matter, any endeavor by humans or animals or, for all we know, plants. (*Culture* has also been defined as the glue that holds an organization together. But can an organization have culture without communication? Which comes first?) A friend who happens to be a professor of business—a technologist, not a linguist—perhaps best answered that question: clear communication enables business to be; without it, there wouldn't be such a thing as business at all. We can legitimately expand "business" to "any organization" or to "all society."

Richard Weaver, in his marvelous book *Ideas Have Consequences*, which was published in 1948 and is as supremely relevant today as it was then, noted that "all metaphysical community depends on the ability of men to understand one another."[2] Business is included, of course, perhaps to a greater extent than we imagine.

Consider the following: if *metaphysical* means "abstract, general reasoning" or "excessively subtle or theoretical," then the business community is the most metaphysical of all communities. Why? Because, despite the best efforts of number crunchers to reduce decisions to mathematical certainty, most decisions are still made by connecting abstract "facts" and drawing conclusions, a process we have labeled "intuition."

Managers I know would agree. They understand at some intuitive level that the very existence of their means of livelihood depends on communication; however, they probably do not understand that communication is the means to their personal success, as well as the success of their organization.

"Bad English makes even the best ideas unbelievable."

Russell E. Eshleman Jr.

The ancients believed that there is a certain divinity in language, that individuals with the power over language are able to influence and control others. (Does that sound like management?) Such individuals were or are either revered or feared or both. Regardless, they are bestowed, rightly or wrongly, with superior insight into the way things actually work or should work.

Jesus is perhaps the most obvious example of an Articulate who was—and still is—both revered and feared; others of lesser but still formidable authority immediately spring to mind. Among them is Socrates and his judicial murder for articulately speaking his thoughts on politics and society—words that were later immortalized in writing by Plato in his *Symposium*. Another example is Abraham Lincoln, who won the presidency by being more articulate than his more experienced (and supposedly more articulate) opponent—how many people remember Stephen A. Douglas?—during public debates, and probably won the "Articulate of the Millennium" award at Gettysburg. (I want to note here that Jesus and Socrates never wrote a word; others, some known to us and some who will be unknown forever, took on that daunting task, for which we can offer only our deepest thanks.)

A personal experience, one that is repeated often, confirms the point: I am approached regularly at parties and other gatherings by individuals, usually strangers, who open the conversation with an admiring look and the statement "I hear that you are a writer." When I admit that I am, the person says something along these lines: "I always wanted to write, but I'm not smart enough," automatically endowing me with reverence based on intelligence and insight that are at least superior to his or hers. That's the revered part of the equation.

Of course, that is a jump in logic that curdles the mind. To prove it, I always point out that I am (or would be if I were so inclined) a lousy brain surgeon or rocket scientist, and that I cannot understand a word written by, for example, Stephen Hawking—even when he dumbs down his thoughts to appeal to a wider audience. I cannot fathom the complexities, some of which I am convinced are perpetrated on unsuspecting readers in a misguided attempt to impress that reverts to irritating pomposity, of many of the faceless financial analysts who toil for my stockbroker. All of these folks are smart in their own ways and in the sense that they can point to high IQs. But let's face it, many of us in the more grounded world must take somebody else's word that he or she is intelligent simply because we have not the slightest clue what he or she is thinking. Is it fair for me to label this individual inarticulate and therefore not so smart after all because he or she can't communicate with me? I think it is. We do that every day, don't we?

I am also often told that I think differently—than whom is never explained. Nevertheless, I always ask, "How do I think differently?" The answer is always, "You see connections among thoughts that I can't." Some people label that skill as weird, lending me an aura of the mysterious, of the occult. That's the feared part of the equation.

"The one basic skill needed in industry is the ability to organize and express ideas in writing and speaking."

Peter Drucker

Simple observations that we call empirical knowledge or existentialism combine with complex statistical studies of articulation to create a clear case for articulation as the one basic skill that drives success, the revered half of the equation.

Richard Weaver reports: "American universities have found that with few exceptions students who display great mastery of words, as evidenced by vocabulary tests and exercises in writing, make the best scholastic records regardless of the department of study they enter. For physics, for chemistry, for engineering—it matters not how superficially unrelated to language the branch of study may be—command of language will prognosticate aptitude. Facility with words bespeaks a capacity to learn relations and grasp concepts; it is a means of access to the complex reality."[3]

Yet such a simple connection seems difficult to grasp for many in academe and business. The dean of a major MBA program told me that the companies that hire his graduates complain bitterly and often that they—the graduates—can't express themselves by either writing or speaking. When I ask if his curriculum includes courses in communications—writing in particular—he stares into his coffee and says yes, one, and it includes six hours (three classes) of writing fundamentals. The remainder of the class focuses on the false god of information technology, which is a false god because it actually deflects students away from thinking about what they are communicating. Spell-check is a particular villain in this regard; it will pass over "its" when "it's" should be used, "god" when "good" is meant, and countless other troublesome words that only the brain can select.

The dean and I both know that even the most gifted teachers cannot teach anything worthwhile about writing in six hours. That's especially true for the many students who learned in the fifth grade that Dick and Jane have a dog named Spot, who haven't been taught even the basics of writing or speaking since (English majors excepted), and who don't have a clue as to why they should be taught the basics now. That seems too much like trying to save the *Titanic* with a bailing bucket, and it seems that we are seriously shortchanging our students.

The entire faculty of the Graduate School of Environmental Science and Management, where I teach, met not long ago to review the 30 or so courses we offer candidates for a master's. All except three of the courses were described as "writing intensive," which, of course, is the subjective judgment of the individual instructors. The head of the department chuckled at that and said, "Maybe we should turn the whole curriculum over to Pete." I am the only instructor of writing, and my course, with some coaching in presentations, is the only one dedicated entirely to communications. The other attendees laughed nervously; amazingly, at least to me, not one approached me after the meeting and asked what he or she could do to help students communicate better.

My students—with undergraduate degrees in geology, biology, botany, and other sciences—think of writing as a nuisance to be endured, perhaps because they haven't a glimmer into how important it is to their academic and business careers, much less to their personal relationships. Many continue on this misguided track even after I point out to them that they spend at least half of their time on the job writing and probably three-fourths of their time communicating in some way—and, therefore, *at least half of their pay is for writing.* You'd be amazed at how astounded they are after they process that simple fact of life. Nevertheless, they haven't devoted a dime's worth of time or money to improve their writing abilities. Why? is a legitimate question with a simple, discouraging answer: none of their teachers or bosses ever explained it to them, and they don't think deeply enough to uncover it themselves.

I also point out that the *interim and most critical* products of the environmental profession/business—and virtually every business—are proposals (people and companies are constantly searching for new sources of money), reports (the routes to the next project or study, still sources of money), and letters (almost all of which are to impress and mine these same sources of money). I call these documents "interim" because they lead, at times via a number of tortuous steps, to the final products: a satisfying and well-paying career and a cleaner environment.

When I expose my students to this new way to perceive their chosen profession as communicators first and scientists in their discipline second, they always fidget a bit and then reply that yes, while their documents are products, they are backed by knowledge of their disciplines. I agree and then ask, "How will anybody know of your knowledge if you can't articulate it?" (Which is my cue to tell them of the turgid and tangled prose my stockbroker's analysts spit out in a futile attempt to convince me to buy whatever it is they're pushing at the moment. I try hard not to buy products pushed by people who are too inarticulate to explain them to me. Don't you?)

I daresay that the environmental business is like most others and that most businesses could be described in the same terms. For example, one manufacturer of electrical equipment confessed to me that employees think of the business as supplying "hardware." They, and their customers, see only the tip of a very deep iceberg because, in fact, at least 75 percent of the cost of hardware is information in many forms, beginning with installation, operations, and safety instructions (reports). Then there's the engineering and scientific knowledge needed (and communicated) to design and build the hardware in the first place (more reports). And, perhaps easiest to forget but equally important, the communicating of all that knowledge to customers so that they can rationally decide on a purchase (letters and proposals, whether written or verbal).

When I point out to the managers that perhaps it would be profitable to train employees to be more articulate, they buy the latest computer. That single, misguided decision accelerates communications and, at the same time according to all sorts of studies, actually increases sloppiness (read "an apparent lack of intelligence"). The net result is less understanding by readers, and this costs an organization big bucks by setting in motion tag games and other activities that seriously erode productivity. (See chapters 10 and 11 for more on this important point.)

A CEO of a small, rapidly growing high-tech company told me that communication among employees is his company's most pressing problem, and it's been exacerbated by computers. "It's too easy to jot down, often carelessly, any thought that comes to mind and pressing 'send all' to cover all the bases, so we get messages we don't need, don't want, and can't understand. How do I get 'clarity' and 'need to know' in their heads?" (My answer to that question was exactly what he didn't want to hear: education, which, of course, requires even more communications.)

"Words are, of course, the most powerful
drugs used by mankind."

Rudyard Kipling

The Johnson O'Connor Research Foundation[4] began its investigations into the link between articulateness and position on the organization's management ladder as far back as 1935, when it tested 100 college seniors, all studying to become business leaders, to quantify their vocabularies (the number of words a person knows the meanings of and can use in communications and thinking).

Vocabulary, the foundation reasoned, is a prerequisite for articulateness, which in turn is a prerequisite for knowledge and insight. To flesh out that concept, we all use words to process information; we think in words most often and use pictures to complement the words. Therefore, we process information more easily and precisely if we know and understand the meanings of more words; we think "better." Elusively simple.

Stated another way, people with larger vocabularies can uncover relationships among ideas/facts/items and then find common ground and deviations from expectations simply because they can think in more words. To take that idea to an extreme, try writing a report or going through an entire day using only, say, 3 or 30 different words. You don't need to try it to know that it would be frustratingly impossible, even more so as you try to express more complex thoughts.

Norman G. Shidle, in his 1965 book, *The Art of Successful Communication*, expanded the thought that people with larger vocabularies are better thinkers when he wrote: "Most important are the rewards (of good communications) manifested in improved abilities to use your mind effectively. These result from practice of the mental disciplines of good communications writing . . . bringing to focus the main ideas of each communication makes one adept in decision-making's first and most vital step."[5]

Psychologists Don H. Hockenbury and Sandra E. Hockenbury expand on this concept: "All our cognitive abilities are involved in understanding and producing language. Using learning and memory, you acquire and remember the meaning of words. You interpret words you hear or read (or see, in the case of American Sign Language) through the use of perception. You use language to help you reason, represent and solve problems, and make decisions."[6] Joan Didion expressed the same thoughts in her brilliant 1968 book, *Slouching Towards Bethlehem*: "I am still committed to the idea that the ability to think for oneself depends upon one's mastery of the language."[7]

To complete the cycle from input to output, persons with larger vocabularies can express themselves more clearly, concisely, and precisely to others—completing our definition of articulate.

Returning to the 1935 O'Connor study, the tested students' careers and incomes were then tracked at regular intervals for more than 20 years; the findings are so absolutely conclusive that they are startling:

- All those tested who scored in the top 10 percent later became executives and enjoyed the highest incomes. The operative word is "all"; there were no exceptions.
- None of those tested who scored in the bottom 25 percent made it to the executive suite or the upper income brackets. The operative word is "none"; there were no exceptions.

At this point I can almost hear some readers muttering that 1935 was a long time ago—business has come a long way, baby—and our computers help us to be articulate now. I answer those skeptics with these rhetorical questions: Is communicating less important now than it was then? If you think so, why do we say so often that we—all of us, not just businesspeople—are living in the information age? Why do we complain about being overwhelmed with information? And if you think computers help you communicate, why do we not understand each other so often? See Chapter 10 for more on this important point and on the huge costs of inarticulation to any organization.

In 1984, the O'Connor Foundation continued its investigations into the reasons for success by testing the vocabularies of 456 company presidents. The results were again sharply conclusive: the vocabularies of presidents are significantly larger than those of other businesspersons (the "norm" group). For example, 90 percent of the presidents scored 180 points out of a perfect 225, while only 60 percent of the norm group did.

Kevin Marks, an early reviewer of this book and a middle manager at Xerox, wrote: "All good managers have this ability [to articulate], which becomes less consistent and noticeable the further down the ranks you go . . . People with aspirations of climbing higher work to be more articulate. They need to properly articulate the company line in any situation, be it to a customer, shareholder, competitor, or employee."

In 1990, the foundation published the results of two follow-on studies. One evaluated the vocabularies of a random sample of 379 managers throughout the United States; another evaluated a sample of 322 professional-level employees of a large manufacturer of cars and trucks.

In general, the managers' vocabularies were smaller than the presidents' studied previously, and many of the managers, perhaps recognizing the need, were working to close the gap by building their vocabularies through careful reading and by playing word games.

The professionals ranged from nonsupervisory personnel to executive vice presidents. In general, those perched on the higher rungs of the corporate ladder had larger vocabularies.

The bottom line is, simply, that articulate people—people with larger vocabularies—are more successful. Their ability to think more clearly by connecting thoughts that may seem to be unrelated at first blush, and then to translate those thoughts and ideas into powerful and effective words is, without doubt, linked to position on any organization's ladder and, of course, to income.

David A. Kay agrees: "An extensive vocabulary and knowledge of the language is the single most important indicator of success . . . regardless of one's interpretation of success: as financial reward, assured social position, or as satisfaction in accomplished and recognized work. Also, high vocabularies are inextricable predictors of success on intelligence tests."[8]

Can 97 percent of executives be wrong?
You make the call.

Ninety-seven percent of the presidents and managers tested are convinced that building vocabularies is extremely or moderately useful for anyone wanting to advance in business or other organizations.

Ninety-eight percent said that vocabulary is extremely or moderately useful for success as an executive, and more than half are increasing their vocabularies in various ways. They know for sure that being articulate is an asset that must be nourished constantly, every day, without letups. They know that being articulate yields increasingly higher returns.

Vocabulary is the precursor/predictor of success; it is also a key to *continuing* success.

"You can't be a doctor . . ."

Bill Cosby, 2004

Comedian and TV personality Bill Cosby got it absolutely right when, in May 2004, he told a group of black leaders that "everybody knows it's important to speak English except these knuckleheads. You can't be a doctor with that kind of crap coming out of your mouth."[9] ("Knuckleheads" refers to black adults and children who refuse to speak standard English for whatever reasons, and "crap" refers to the nonstandard English of some black people; but let's be clear here, these terms could refer to those of any race.)

Cosby "is trying to protect the future of blacks, especially of the younger generation," reported Thomas Sowell, a senior fellow of the Hoover Institution and a syndicated columnist who also happens to be black.[10] Cosby backs up his beliefs by giving generously to promote black education and by actually paying for the higher educations of several black scholars selected for their promising academic records.

The most surprising reaction (to me) to Cosby's words came from the black "leadership." The heads of the National Association for the Advancement of Colored Persons and its Legal Defense Fund, and the president of Howard University were stone-faced. I think they should have applauded vigorously. And columnist Earl Ofari Hutchinson opined that what people "heard from [Cosby] only reinforces negative beliefs about the black poor."[11]

Maybe they left the applause to Jesse Jackson. I watched him on CNN agree with Cosby and state several times that Cosby's message was upbeat and a challenge to all blacks to study more than others, regardless of race, simply because blacks are starting behind in the search for success.

Forget race. Cosby's message applies to all of us.[12]

> *"This book is about you and your future."*
>
> Pete Geissler, 2006

I've drawn three major conclusions from all my observations and the few extant studies that connect articulation to success. First, articulation, combined with competence in a person's regular discipline (which, of course, is related to articulation as well, an important connection that Richard Weaver made years ago and which I reported on earlier in this chapter), is a major driver of success as measured by position on the organizational ladder and income.

In addition, articulation is a major reason for remaining at that position. An inarticulate person who somehow rose to a managerial level for whatever reason most likely has hit his or her ceiling and may in fact be ousted. And, topping off the benefits, articulation is key to happiness.

The remainder of the book brings these and other abstractions to the very thoughtful personalities of those I call the Articulates. Managers of various stripes and levels will tell you, in their own articulate words, how being articulate shaped their lives and their organizations, why they value articulate employees, and more.

I think you'll enjoy and profit from meeting these people, all accomplishers in their own ways. I know that I did.

● ● ● ●

A few early and insightful reviewers of the premise and promise of this book were quick to point out the chicken-and-egg conundrum I've created: which came first on the road to success, proficiency in a person's main discipline such as engineering or law, or proficiency in the language?

They miss the point: *both proficiencies are needed in equal doses*; but we don't teach them with equal emphasis, and we don't teach them in the proper sequence. In short, our education system is misdirected, even backward. Consider that we learn to read and write in the early grades because, at that time in our cerebral development, our educators recognize that teaching other subjects would be futile. If students cannot articulate what they've learned, educators reason, they can't ask intelligent questions to fill in the gaps of what they haven't learned.

Then, in high school, we are told to choose a major, which is tantamount to choosing our life's work. Studies are focused on that major, and the language plays second fiddle. The trend continues in college, where studies of the language are de-emphasized even more.

The result is college graduates who haven't studied the language for more than five years, and then only cursorily. They hit the working world totally unaware of the need for articulation and virtually unable to be articulate without further education—the reason that so many universities and private charm schools offer such programs.

Earl Nightingale, in a marvelous audiocassette called *The Only Thing You Cannot Hide*, points out that "a person should begin with the study of his language, and then study his area of interest. These two steps, in that order, can move us right up there, to the top of the [social and economic] pyramid . . . it is the ability to use our language that will control, to a great extent, the amount of money we will earn during our lifetimes."[13] See what I mean by "backward"?

John Yasinsky, profiled in Chapter 4, is undoubtedly a highly competent physicist. Would he have found his way to the top of several large corporations and served as a board member of a liberal arts college if he had not been articulate as well? He answers that query with an emphatic no. I'm betting you'll agree with him after you've read his story.

However, could he have been a top physicist without being articulate? Perhaps. But his considerable talents as a manager would have never been tapped, and his income would surely have been less.

Other reviewers complain that I am somehow encouraging and approving the division or schism based on income in our country that is already too wide. Again, they miss an important point: I didn't create the divide; I am merely pointing out that it's real, it's been around for a while (witness the 1935 study described earlier in this chapter), and it's worldwide. All of us on this planet are in the information age, and we can't do a thing about it.

I bristle when I hear that I am creating another societal division when in fact I am trying to narrow or eliminate the division between the haves and the have nots. Everybody, and I do mean everybody, can improve his or her vocabulary, thinking, and incomes[14]—narrowing economic divisions. Ambitious and creative individuals would benefit, of course, but that's only the tip of a very deep iceberg: our entire society would benefit with better-informed voters who would elect more responsible and responsive leaders. And our economy would take off with a serious competitive advantage in the global marketplace that would be created and sustained by information and superior abilities to put it to work.

Still other reviewers are disturbed that articulation has been harnessed for evil purposes throughout man's sordid history and could be again. True, articulation is a weapon, as such despots as Hitler and Stalin knew only too well. Nevertheless, I daresay without a scintilla of scientific or statistical evidence that many more people have used articulation for just and moral purposes than not. They just don't get the headlines from media dedicated to reporting crises and scares.

I return to the purpose of this book: to point out that articulation is linked directly and tightly to success in business and other pursuits acceptable to our society.

Notes

1. My apologies to such classic thinkers like Francis Bacon, who perhaps was the first, in 1597, to write "Knowledge is power," and to Samuel Johnson, who later expressed the same thought sometime in the mid-1700s: "Knowledge is more than equivalent to force." Both stole the idea from the anonymous writer(s) of Proverbs 25:5, who centuries earlier wrote: "A wise man is strong; yea, a man of knowledge increaseth strength."
2. Richard M. Weaver, *Ideas Have Consequences* (Chicago: University of Chicago Press, 1948), p. 148.
3. See note 2, pp. 161, 162.
4. The Johnson O'Connor Research Foundation is headquartered in New York City and operates branch offices in 10 other cities in the United States. Since the early 1930s the foundation's experts have studied the relationships of vocabulary and cognitive style to success as defined by position on the executive ladder.

5. Norman G. Shidle, *The Art of Successful Communication* (New York: McGraw-Hill, 1965), pp. 258–259.

6. Don H. Hockenbury and Sandra E. Hockenbury, *Psychology*, 3rd ed. (New York: Worth Publishers, 2003), p. 293.

7. Joan Didion, *Slouching Towards Bethlehem* (New York: Farrar, Straus & Giroux, 1968).

8. Mr. Kay is renowned for his research into educational testing. He was associated for 35 years with the Johnson O'Connor Research Foundation and is currently president of WordSmart Educational Technology, which he founded in 1993. WordSmart software has been recognized and widely praised for its success in increasing vocabularies of students and others of all ages.

9. "Politicizing English," *Pittsburgh Tribune Review*, June 5, 2004, p. A7.

10. Thomas Sowell, "Bravo for the 60s," *Pittsburgh Tribune Review*, May 27, 2004, p. A17.

11. Earl Ofari Hutchinson, "Stop Blaming the Victim," *Pittsburgh Tribune Review*, July 18, 2004, p. F4. Hutchinson is a political analyst and the author of *The Crisis in Black and Black*.

12. The editors of the *Pittsburgh Tribune Review* opined on September 23, 2004, in a short piece titled "Left Behind by Illiteracy" that "fifty three percent of working-class adults in Los Angeles are illiterate to the extent that they can't cope with street signs, employment applications, or utility bills. These 3.8 million people are a small portion of the 48 percent of adult Americans who can't read and write English well enough *to have a shot at the good life*." (emphasis mine)

13. Earl Nightingale, *The Only Thing You Cannot Hide* in *Lead the Field*, a series of audiocassettes (Chicago: Nightingale-Conant, 2002).

14. The Johnson O'Connor Research Foundation has demonstrated that intelligence, rather than being fixed at birth, is in fact somewhat malleable. It can be improved because it is a dynamic combination of innate aptitudes and learned information. And anyone can expand his or her vocabulary; see Chapter 13 for suggestions.

3

CLOWT, and How You Can Get It

The five habits of very successful Articulates that can easily and quickly be yours.

All the Articulates profiled in Part II of this book are addicted to five basic behaviors that govern their business and personal lives: compartmentalize, listen, organize, write, test (CLOWT). I've grouped these behaviors by input (collecting and processing information) and output (writing, speaking, and testing the message).

The few Also-Rans discussed and dissed in Chapter 6 fail disastrously to meet even the basic standards for many, if not most, of the five behaviors. Their failures have, in some cases, shortened careers or led to the demise of their companies.

The profiles of the Articulates are intended to prod readers to recognize certain behaviors in themselves and to emulate other individuals where appropriate. In a sense, I am setting up role models. The profiles of the Also-Rans are intended to point out behaviors to avoid—the anti role models.

The five behaviors of CLOWT are discussed in the following sections.

INPUT

1. Compartmentalize

Train your mind to make sudden starts and stops. *Compartmental-ize*—the admiring media popularized the long-standing term during Bill Clinton's tenure as president—is the ability to concentrate solely on the matter at hand and to move seamlessly from one matter to another. Perhaps it has been replaced recently by *multitasking*, the supposed ability to concentrate on more than one matter at a time, which is an illusion; nobody can truly focus on two cerebral tasks simultaneously. The operative words are "focus" and "cerebral."

If you don't believe that—and many of my peers fall into that trap simply because they are addicted to what they think of as multitasking—consider that a student of mine argued that multitasking was possible. He then started to read in class as I was professing (reinforcing what I've said too often: that paying attention is the scarcest skill). I stopped talking and waited in silence as he read. When he finally realized that something was amiss, he looked up from his reading. I asked him what I had been saying. He had no idea. "Why weren't you multitasking?" I asked. He blushed, so I knew that he and the other students got the point.

Another example is a current TV ad for an insurance company. The very serious announcer drones in a laconic tone that we mistakenly take for seriousness: multitasking; we all do it. We're on our cell phones, we drink coffee as we drive, and so on. Then he tells us how such behavior causes accidents and raises the cost of insurance. Tell me this: if multitasking is possible, why can't we concentrate on driving while doing all those other simple things?

2. Listen

Train your mind to slow down the speed of thinking (more than 500 words a minute) to the speed of talking (about 125 words a minute). In essence, your brain gives you some 400 words a minute of excess capacity while you're listening to someone else, so you can wander off to any other subject that suits your fancy. That's trouble in the making (called inattention), and Articulates avoid it by consciously tapping the brakes and slowing down. Habits to do so include taking notes, rephrasing what you hear, and asking the speaker to rephrase what he or she said. Excess capacity isn't all bad. For example, it's great when you're listening to yourself (called thinking) or when you don't want to hear what someone else is saying. (Face it, it happens.)

Articulates never interrupt or finish the sentences of those who are speaking to them, and they avoid people who do. They know that such people are using their excess brain capacity to think about something other than what's being said: they aren't paying attention. Jim Browne, profiled in Chapter 5, places such a high priority on his employees' ability to listen that he won't hire an interrupter or a finisher (a trait that usually reveals itself during the initial interview). And I advise my students not to become involved with one and, especially, not to marry one; it guarantees a lifetime of not being heard (also known as being ignored).

3. Organize

Articulates organize their thoughts as they listen (whether to others or to themselves); they group details, often subconsciously, to create larger abstractions that writers sometimes label "the grander ideas," which can be connected and analyzed, often in new ways that others find strange, surreal, or just plain inaccessible. The pivotal importance of vocabulary enters the process here for the first time, as words are used to connect thoughts—and the more words, the merrier.

OUTPUT

4. Write

Applying the disciplines of writing, particularly those that force logical progressions and groupings, shapes messages that are more understandable, whether those messages are sent via printed or spoken words. For those of you who tripped over "spoken," the answer is yes, writing is a prerequisite for speaking in formal settings.

Writing, in its essence, is primarily an exercise in discovering and conveying logic, and cleansing and clarifying our thoughts; it is the way we watch ourselves think. A number of well-known writers have expressed this concept in their own ways. Isaac Asimov, for example, said, "Thinking is the activity I love best, and writing to me is thinking through my fingers." Nadine Gordimer said, "Writing is making sense of life," and Henry Miller added, "Writing, like life itself, is a voyage of discovery."[1]

William Zinsser, in his book *Writing to Learn*, expanded the idea greatly when he wrote: "Finally, in the national furor over why Johnny can't write, let's not forget to ask why Johnny can't learn. The two are connected. Writing organizes and clarifies our thoughts. Writing is how we think our way into a subject and make it our own. Writing enables us to find out what we know—and what we don't know—about whatever we're trying to learn. Putting an idea into written words is like defrosting a windshield: The idea, so vague out there in the murk, slowly begins to gather itself into a sensible shape. Whatever we write—a memo, a letter, a note to the baby-sitter—all of us know this moment of finding out what we really want to say by trying in writing to say it."[2]

On a more personal note, several of my clients retain me and other writers primarily because we help them think, secondarily to help them express thoughts, and they are well aware that the two are connected so tightly as to be one. One client has often told me that my greatest value to him is my annoying habit of asking, "Do you really want to say that to this audience?" It forces him to think and rethink the content, structure, and tone of his message. Lee Iacocca recognized the value of writing as a discipline when he said, "In conversation, you can get away with vagueness and nonsense, often without even realizing it. But there's something about putting your thoughts on paper that forces you to get down to specifics. That way it's harder to deceive yourself—or anybody else."

A professor of environmental science at the university where I teach understands this principle well; he insists on good writing from his students before he insists on good science. He sees clear writing as the reflection of clear thinking and, therefore, the key to learning. And Joe D, whom you'll meet in Chapter 8, bases his hiring decisions first on candidates' abilities to write and second on their abilities to engineer. "I can teach them to be better engineers," he says, "but I don't know how to teach them to be better writers."

Others argue that managers, particularly those at or near the top of their organizations, don't need to write or learn the disciplines of writing; they can call on their cadre of writers toiling in advertising, public relations, and technical writing groups. The argument is spurious: the computer has literally forced managers to become keyboardists (today's euphemism for typists), and, more importantly, those same managers can benefit from applying the disciplines of writing to their messages.

5. Test

All messages in business are purposeful; they have jobs to do, so they have job descriptions. Stated another way, messages are employed, just as any person is employed, to contribute positively to the organization.[3] Defining that job (contribution) is the first step in defining the message; deciding if the purpose was met is the last step, the test of its effectiveness.

The job of all communications in business is to persuade. My colleagues, particularly those at Carnegie Mellon University, and many of the engineers who attend my seminars argue that "inform" is equally important.

Baloney. The purpose of every one of the three million words I have written for business was to persuade—to persuade customers to buy a product or service, to persuade stock analysts to write reports favorable to a company's outlook and raise stock prices, to convince employees to become part of the organization's culture, and so on.

John Yasinsky started his turnaround of GenCorp by first convincing all employees that the company was in trouble and then instructing each employee to change his or her behavior to turn the tide. He started with a purpose and ended by measuring his success at meeting it. Georgia Berner, profiled in Chapter 9, used her persuasive powers to convince an employee working as a clerk to accept the position of manager of production. Jim Browne, as described in Chapter 5, learned and applied the powers of subtle persuasion to build a successful and growing business. You'll find many other examples throughout this book.

Notes

1. Jon Winokur, *W.O.W. Writers on Writing* (Philadelphia: Running Press, 1990), pp. 317, 342, 344.
2. William Zinsser, *Writing to Learn* (New York: Harper and Row, 1988), p. 16. Zinsser is the author of some 13 books, including *On Writing Well, Writing to Learn,* and *Writing with a Word Processor*—all respected by professional writers and teachers of writing at many levels. He also taught writing at Yale University.
3. Examples abound of communications that have contributed negatively; I've noted a few in Chapter 10, "The High Costs of Inarticulation," and Chapter 11, "The High Profits of Articulation." I'm sure that readers can come up with countless other examples, both positive and negative, from their own experiences.

PART II

PROFILES OF
PRACTITIONERS

One example is worth a thousand theories.

4 John Yasinsky

*The scientist as CEO, and his
four phases toward articulation.*

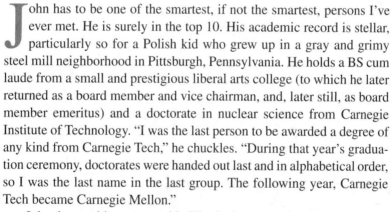

John has to be one of the smartest, if not the smartest, persons I've
ever met. He is surely in the top 10. His academic record is stellar,
particularly so for a Polish kid who grew up in a gray and grimy
steel mill neighborhood in Pittsburgh, Pennsylvania. He holds a BS cum
laude from a small and prestigious liberal arts college (to which he later
returned as a board member and vice chairman, and, later still, as board
member emeritus) and a doctorate in nuclear science from Carnegie
Institute of Technology. "I was the last person to be awarded a degree of
any kind from Carnegie Tech," he chuckles. "During that year's gradua-
tion ceremony, doctorates were handed out last and in alphabetical order,
so I was the last name in the last group. The following year, Carnegie
Tech became Carnegie Mellon."

John began his career with Westinghouse at its Naval Nuclear
Power Laboratory long before managers at Westinghouse or anybody
else realized his potential. The nuclear power business was approaching
its zenith and flexing its muscles, and Westinghouse, as the worldwide
leader in design and development, needed all the talent, untested or sea-
soned, it could muster.

John fit the profile of the perfect employee for a business that prized
technical competence as much as the ability to translate technology to
words that, he joked often, "even a busy bureaucrat who couldn't pass
high-school physics could understand." He brought many other assets

to the party as well. He was tall, Hollywood-handsome, obviously intelligent way beyond the norm, quietly thoughtful, soft-spoken, and a bit impatient to move ahead and up. Here was a man who could be counted on to represent the company with class and dignity in any situation.

He was quickly labeled a "comer" by top management in the business unit and at corporate headquarters and moved rapidly to positions of ever-increasing responsibility and widening spans of control. Then outside forces intervened, and he left Westinghouse to become a successful CEO of a large and diversified manufacturing company in need of major surgery.

THE EARLY YEARS

"When I first joined Westinghouse I was a pure scientist without any management responsibilities, and I thought at the time that science would be my career. My abilities to articulate weren't tested very severely. In essence, I communicated technology to technologists, a narrow subject to an audience with narrow interests. On top of that, I had the luxury of all sorts of time and space to convey my message. Being concise wasn't important; it took a backseat to being complete, maybe too complete. One result was that I didn't learn to find my central idea and get to it in a hurry, and I probably told my audiences more than they wanted or needed to know.

"Despite this glaring deficit, during my first 10 years at the Westinghouse Bettis Atomic Power Laboratory I authored and published 50 or 60 technical articles and gave countless presentations at various conferences and other venues.

"Then disillusionment set in. I became bored with the sameness of the subject and tone of my communications, and realized I had to branch out, expand my horizons, and start swimming in a bigger pond. Suddenly I decided that I didn't want to confine my life solely to science; I wanted someday to manage, to lead, to be a CEO of a large company."

CRAMMING 10 YEARS INTO 1
AT THE WHITE HOUSE

"So, in the early seventies and with the full support of Westinghouse, I and 3500 others from a wide range of other firms and organizations applied to become White House Fellows. Honestly, I never thought in my wildest dreams that I would be one of the 14 selected for this signal honor, but I was.

"I'll never forget the final step in the selection process. Thirty-five survivors of the rigorous selection process were invited to a weekend in Washington, where we were interviewed intensely by the President's Commission on White House Fellows. Then, on Sunday evening, an anonymous somebody slid an envelope under our hotel doors. Inside was our acceptance or rejection. Those who were accepted were invited, along with our spouses, to meet President Nixon the next afternoon for an official greeting and congratulations. I immediately called my wife with the news, and she was on the morning plane. As an aside, she had purchased a dress for the occasion but hadn't removed the price tag just in case she had to return it. She displayed both her confidence and caution at the same time.

"I'm pretty certain that being somewhat articulate was a significant, perhaps deciding, factor in my selection; I'll never know for sure. Nevertheless, that year was a turning point in my life. I figure I crammed 10 years of unbelievable experience and knowledge into 1 year, and was thrust into the second phase on the road to my becoming an Articulate.

"My office during that year was within spitting distance to several of President Nixon's insider group. I met and interacted with both the famous and infamous, many of who became household names: Chuck Colson, Jeb McGruder, Bob Haldemann, Henry Kissinger, and others. I traveled to the major capitals of the world, met heads of state in dozens of countries, and participated in numerous international initiatives such as the opening of trade with the People's Republic of China. And I matured as I listened and absorbed how successful and powerful people behaved, particularly how they were able—or unable, in some cases—to communicate their points of view on complex issues to a wide range of audiences."

"Tell me, John," I asked, "who were the best and worst articulators in that elite group?"

"I think my answer will surprise you. Despite his heavy accent and massive ego, Henry Kissinger was, and probably still is, marvelously articulate. I was somewhat awed by his uncanny ability to boil down a huge amount of complex information to its essence, and then to communicate that essence logically and understandably in the shortest possible time. Time, so important in business, is, perhaps, even more important at high levels of government, where the pace always seems to border on frantic.

"Let me give you an example of Kissinger's skill. Nixon is often credited with single-handedly opening China to trade and diplomatic relations with the U.S. after about four decades of being closed, but I give more credit to Kissinger. He came up with the initial idea, researched the political and economic consequences, achieved consensus support of other senior officials, put together the plan of action, and convinced Nixon to go ahead. I often wonder how many people today, more than 30 years later, understand how that one decision changed the course of the global economy, how it started the monumental movement we call globalization, and how important effective communications was to the outcome.

"On the negative side of the articulation coin are all the blokes who were involved with Watergate. What they did was legally and morally indefensible, as we all know. It's also a failure in planning and articulation. While they planned the caper itself very well, they neglected to foresee the ramifications if they were caught. I found it downright painful to watch them try to talk their way out of that mess with denial, waffling, resisting . . . all words that boil down to mendacity of the worst kind. We all know the story and its ending. This experience taught me a lesson that I have never forgotten: communications fail miserably when they are based on dishonesty.

"I put Pete Peterson, the secretary of commerce at the time, in the middle, somewhere between a successful and unsuccessful articulator, specifically on the issue of energy independence. He saw, a few years before the first oil embargo in 1973, that the country was too dependent on imported oil, and he told everyone who would listen that trouble was on the horizon. I think he told the story very clearly but obviously not convincingly because nothing was done to prevent the embargoes, and nothing significant is being done now to prevent a repeat that is sure to be even more disruptive. On this issue, Peterson was a good example of a leader who, as an individual, communicated clearly and cogently, yet his efforts were never effective enough to establish the consensus among high-level decision makers that is needed for them to act. I believe that this ability to create consensus is a key element of being an Articulate and was key to my success at GenCorp.

"Anyway, my year as a White House Fellow opened my eyes to the huge importance of communications, of articulation, and that drastically altered the way I wanted to communicate. Perhaps the biggest changes were the needs to be concise and germane to my audience: I no longer had unlimited time and space in which to convey my message, and I no longer had a homogeneous audience. Instead, I was literally forced to condense huge ideas and issues to a few sentences of type or a few minutes of talk. And I had to do that for all sorts of expert and novice audiences. I learned to shape and compress messages in ways that I never dreamed possible, and I developed, for the first time in my life, the confidence needed to do it well."

ONCE I SAW PARIS . . .

"That combination of skill and confidence served me well when I returned to Westinghouse, where I was first offered a top management job at the laboratory in which I had worked previously as a scientist. What's that old saying along the lines of 'once they've seen Paris, it's tough to bring 'em back to the farm'? I had seen Paris, and I wanted a job with far broader responsibilities, a job that demanded that I use my newfound articulation along with my established expertise as a nuclear scientist.

"I explained that to my superiors at Westinghouse, and they appointed me a top manager of the growing advanced nuclear power group, starting me on phase three of my development as a leader, executive, and Articulate. I was soon named leader of a team of engineers, scientists, and support personnel charged with developing a new type of nuclear reactor called 'the breeder.' The reactor, relying on the complex laws of nuclear physics, could make more fuel than it used as it went about its business of making heat that would eventually be converted to electricity.

"My annual development budget for the breeder grew rapidly to $50 million and more, a good indication of the high priority placed on the project by Westinghouse and the federal government. During this time, I had new opportunities to utilize and further develop my articulation skills with an even more challenging and diverse audience, the U.S. Congress. I led the effort to communicate the nation's need for the breeder to congressional committees that funded such programs. Following success in the congressional arena, I was asked to lead Westinghouse's efforts to communicate the need for nuclear power in the nation's energy mix, a unique opportunity.

"That's when we met, Pete. We worked together on all sorts of position papers, presentations, magazine articles, and other pieces for readers ranging from homeowners to physicists to legislators. I traveled around the country to appear on national TV shows such as *MacNeil/ Lehrer* and *AM America*, to be interviewed on dozens of TV and radio programs, and to sit on countless panel discussions.

"Development of the breeder and our message about the need for nuclear power were progressing quite nicely when the Three Mile Island and Chernobyl incidents helped to slow down the entire nuclear power business, and finally to bring it to its knees. Funding for the breeder and orders for conventional plants stopped. We turned to communicating other messages about energy that were germane to the Westinghouse portfolio, including a position paper and presentation on the need to revive nuclear energy as an integral piece of the nation's total energy mix. They were to be used by Westinghouse lobbyists in DC when they talked to legislators and their aides."

▶ COMPARTMENTALIZE, LISTEN, THINK, WRITE, SPEAK . . . IN THAT ORDER

I picked up the story at this point: "John, you were very, very busy at that time, and I think a couple of incidents that stick in my mind will illustrate your style very nicely.

"One morning we met in your office to go over progress on the lobbying piece, mainly how I was developing the logic. When I got there you were winding down a very intense meeting with your boss, and I waited outside your door. When your boss left, he nodded at me and I could see the tension in his face, so I knew that you were under some sort of gun.

"I knew then that I had exactly the 15 minutes that you had given the meeting—overruns weren't in the cards—so I said good morning and got right down to business. You immediately settled in to our meeting and forgot, or at least seemed to forget, what had happened before. Honestly, it was an impressive turnaround, the quickest 180 in history."

"I remember that morning clearly," John said. "I was being pressured hard to quickly show more profit from the divisions I managed, and I couldn't see how within the time frame he established. My boss wasn't happy. Those were trying times for the company, and little did we know that more trying times were just ahead. By the way, I really did forget the earlier meeting as soon as you walked in the office; it's one of my gifts, the way I can move from one subject to another and not miss a beat."

"Here's another time you showed that gift. You were your usual busy self and I needed more time than I could get in your office so I invited you to lunch. I sent the papers I wanted to review to your office early in the morning, just in case you had the time to look at them before we met. Then, to cover my bases, I got to the restaurant a few minutes early and arranged the papers in the order in which I wanted to discuss them. You were a bit late, obviously harried, sat down, and went to work. No looking back for you."

"In the early to mid-1980s I was given the opportunity to move beyond the nuclear power business, where my nuclear background was always there as a foundation, or safety net. My new and broader challenges involved power generation, environmental services, a wide array of industrial businesses, and the corporation's international business that was spread throughout 45 countries.

"These new challenges gave me numerous fresh opportunities to utilize my expanding articulation skills to pull diverse groups of fellow managers, employees, partners, and customers together to achieve business successes in new arenas. Solving serious problems, turning around underperforming businesses, and winning major new contracts during this period taught me another crucial lesson: success is feasible only through a strong organization of outstanding people who are driven by leadership, and leadership is founded on effective communications. And, to expand on that thought a bit, effective communications are needed to change cultures and achieve alignment of priorities, objectives, and actions from top to bottom of the organization.

"When I left Westinghouse, in 1993, I was group vice president in charge of about one-third of the corporation. The opportunities and experience that I gained during 30 years with Westinghouse gave me the confidence and tools I believed I needed to become a successful CEO at GenCorp, as you'll see later."

THE FINAL PHASE AND THE GENCORP YEARS

"As you can well imagine, as my career with Westinghouse progressed I had absolutely solidified my desire to become a CEO of a large company. When the Westinghouse board brought in a CEO from outside the company, I knew that I had to look elsewhere and started to listen carefully to the headhunters that called. One told me about GenCorp and its need for a CEO who could change the troubled company into a strong and growing industrial leader. The GenCorp board made it very clear to me that they did not want a caretaker; instead, they wanted a change leader.

"Given my recent experience at Westinghouse, the job was a natural fit for me, and I began the final phase of my career. It placed far higher priorities and demands on articulation than ever before.

"GenCorp at that time—the early to mid-nineties—was in trouble. Revenues and earnings had declined for several years, bonds were rated 'junk,' the balance sheet was highly leveraged, and environmental liabilities were large and uncapped. As if that weren't enough, employee morale was low, to a great extent because top execs had not, or perhaps could not, articulate the overall seriousness of the problems the company faced, and the strategies that could solve them and change the direction of the company. All levels of employees, top execs right down to those on the factory floors, weren't focused on common goals. The company and its employees bordered on rudderless."

CARTE BLANCHE AND THE HARD AND SOFT SIDES OF LEADERSHIP

"I mentioned earlier that I had formulated some pretty firm ideas about culture and leadership when I was at Westinghouse. Well, the culture at Westinghouse made it difficult to implement the many changes I believed were necessary. In contrast, GenCorp's board gave me carte blanche to do whatever I thought was needed. Articulation—not only mine, but also of all my direct team and all other managers—played a key role.

"I have many positive memories from my years at Westinghouse, and I'm particularly thankful for the opportunities I was given that allowed me to develop my beliefs and skills concerning management, leadership, and articulation. One strong belief I developed was that there are two sides of the management/leadership continuum: 'hard' and 'soft.' On the hard side are such things as vision, strategy, technical and professional skills, control processes, and capital. On the soft side are values, behavior, recognition and reward, motivation, and alignment, among others.

"I believe that successful managers or leaders must effectively integrate the two sides. I find it unfortunate that often the soft side is neglected or minimized, which can be destructive to any organization.

The reason is simplicity itself: soft-side attributes are hard wired to changing an existing culture, then replacing it with the culture necessary to solidify the changes needed on the hard side.

"I spent the first several months of my tenure as CEO studying where the company was, including its strengths and weaknesses on both the hard and soft sides of the management/leadership continuum. Then I defined where we need to be and how to get there.

"As a necessary beginning, I visited every office and plant in the company. I explained to all employees, from managers to janitors, that the company faced a severe crisis, why and how it developed, what had to change if their jobs were to be saved, and what I expected each of them to do.

"The content and urgent tone of the message shocked many employees, especially the last part—what I expected each of them to do. Too many employees are convinced that they are either too high in the organization or too important to worry about changing, or are too low to be part of either the problem or the solution. I had to convince them otherwise and get everyone's behavior, top to bottom, aligned in strategic direction and tactical action."

ARTICULATION AS KEY TO CULTURAL CHANGE

"The only way to achieve alignment and cultural change was through continued and effective articulation. This may have been the toughest communications challenge of my career, and, again, I approached it from experience. Over the years, I had come to believe that the culture I want can be defined by the set of behaviors I expect every employee to demonstrate and live until they are habituated; that is, they are integrated naturally into everyday activities. When they are, we will have achieved the new culture needed to effectively drive change.

"My staff and I established such a set of Behavioral Expectations (BE) that became prerequisites if jobs and the company were to BE. Simply stated, the behaviors, all of them dependent on articulation to some extent, are:

- BE open to change.
- BE candid, and BE courageous in expressing convictions.
- BE substantive, not shallow.
- BE a constructive critic, and always BE loyal.

- BE competitive, and always BE a willing and cooperative team member.
- BE responsive to suggestions for improvement.
- BE accountable, and BE rewarded and punished appropriately.
- BE passionately committed to continuous improvement.
- BE sensitive to and respectful of people.
- BE aware of objectives and priorities, and act accordingly.
- BE credible, and show your credibility with outstanding performance.

ALIGNMENT DRIVES THE MESSAGE

"I knew that I had to drive the message down to the very first rungs on the corporate ladder; if I didn't, nothing would change. I knew too that driving it to all levels in one fell swoop was unrealistic, that I had to do it one level at a time, and I had to assign responsibilities to get it done.

"I started with my executive staff, most of whom I had selected for their management and articulation skills. They in turn conveyed the message to their direct reports, and so on. The result was employees at every level who understood, clearly and specifically, why we must change, what we are committed to achieve (behavior, vision, strategy, objectives), how this will be achieved, what their individual and group roles were in this change process, and how they will be evaluated.

"I call that process of driving the message to all levels of the organization 'alignment,' because the end result is that all employees are aligned with the same behaviors and goals—they all become part of the same culture and work to meet the same objectives. It can't happen without articulation."

THE PAST WAS PROLOGUE

"Tell me, John, when did you realize that being articulate is key to your success and the success of your organization?"

"I never stopped learning this lesson, which I based on observations: articulate people are clearly more likely to meet their personal and professional goals than inarticulate people, who are rightly dubbed 'Also-Rans' in this book. I guess I started to learn that lesson, which seems so simple in retrospect, while growing up in a working-class neighborhood on the hills above the Pittsburgh steel mills and working in the mills during summer vacations from school.

"The mill workers were a rough bunch, and their language was, well, colorful and colloquial, to be polite. Which is certainly understandable: the teachers at my small school knew that many of the students would end up working in the mill, and you can be a good steel worker without knowing a thing about nouns and verbs or Shakespeare or Shelley. So naturally the focus of our education was simply to 'work hard.'

"The engineers and managers—they were a different breed. Those at the mill site and in headquarters had graduated from college, most of them as engineers, and they had at least been exposed to standard English. I noticed right away that they talked to the mill workers in one way, and to other managers in another, especially those from the head office when they visited. They used bigger words, technical words, and, I think, fewer words to make their points.

"Of course, I noticed that the engineers and managers lived in bigger houses and drove bigger cars, and, impressionable youngster that I was, I wanted to be like them. So I started to study on my own, and I was lucky enough to have parents and a teacher who encouraged me. I was shaped for life by their values, and I thank them for that."

LESSONS LEARNED

"I believe strongly that articulation as defined in this book is one of several skills that are necessary for success at the management level of any organization.

"I include in my definition of Articulate the abilities to organize, package, and deliver the communications at the right time and place. Clearly, however, articulation must be supplemented by and combined with expertise and experience in other disciplines. Management is not divided into separate rooms; it is not a hundred rooms inhabited by strangers; it's all one house whose front door is opened by articulation.

"The opportunity to combine articulation with other skills was critically important to my career growth and success as a White House Fellow, a scientist and senior executive at Westinghouse, and later as CEO of GenCorp. I recognized the importance of this basic truth when I joined GenCorp and formed my executive team. I selected members first and foremost for their relevant expertise and experience, followed closely for their abilities to articulate. Then, to hone their articulation skills with a variety of audiences ranging from employees, customers, investors, suppliers, and partners, I brought in professionals to train them. As I mentioned earlier, GenCorp would survive only if all employees were part of the same culture and were fully aligned in executing our overall business plan, and that required the clearest possible communications.

"It worked. Five years after we began our journey of change, Gen-Corp was a healthy, growing company with an investment-grade balance sheet, well-defined and funded environmental liabilities, and leading market share positions. Over the five years, earnings grew at a compound annual rate in excess of 15 percent, and our stock price rose more than 300 percent as investors saw positive changes throughout the company.

"This success was the direct result of employees' willingness and desire to respond positively to my call for change, a call which they heard and heeded because it had been articulated effectively. I thank them and our other stakeholders."

5 Jim Browne

*From sledgehammer to kid glove
in one diverse career.*

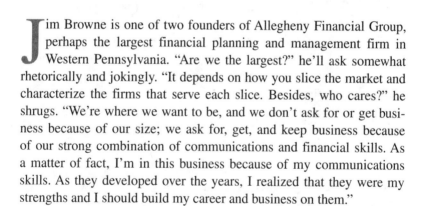

Jim Browne is one of two founders of Allegheny Financial Group, perhaps the largest financial planning and management firm in Western Pennsylvania. "Are we the largest?" he'll ask somewhat rhetorically and jokingly. "It depends on how you slice the market and characterize the firms that serve each slice. Besides, who cares?" he shrugs. "We're where we want to be, and we don't ask for or get business because of our size; we ask for, get, and keep business because of our strong combination of communications and financial skills. As a matter of fact, I'm in this business because of my communications skills. As they developed over the years, I realized that they were my strengths and I should build my career and business on them."

HEAR, LISTEN, UNDERSTAND—THEN RESPOND IN WAYS THAT TOUCH

"Our business is very personal. I know, just about every business in every SIC code can sing that same tune. I'm biased, I'm sure, but I think that our business is more personal than most. Think about it: few things are closer to the hearts and minds of most people than their finances. To take that thought further: finances are either the first or second reasons behind a divorce, and aging parents rarely divulge their worth to their

41

grown children any more than they would divulge, say, the first time they necked in the backseat of Grampa's car. It's difficult to get more personal than that.

"Communications skills and articulation are pretty much one and the same in my mind, and I think of them as part of a larger idea that I call interpersonal skills. In fact, I see all those skills as kissin' cousins to CLOWT that was described in Chapter 3, and just as much of a sequence of events, or process, with input and output sides. I just use different words—words that resonate with me—to say the same thing.

"On the input side are hear, listen, and understand—the three stages of increasing depth in the necessary process of getting to know, really know, a client or any person, for that matter. I think of 'hear' as the first sounds that grab my attention . . . 'listen' as collecting information . . . and 'understand' as putting together the ideas, concepts, wishes, and needs to form a cohesive picture of a human being that we in business label with the anonymous 'client.' I stick to that sequence intuitively, and I expect the 13 members of my immediate team to stick to it as well.

"Pete, you're absolutely correct when you say that vocabulary is the basis for articulation and—you've made a very important point here—thinking. We hear, listen, and understand each other using words, and we connect ideas using words. As the connections grow more complex, we need more words, a direct relationship that I really didn't make until I read your premise."

"I like the sound of your goal for the output side of articulation: respond in ways that touch. Can you expand that idea?"

"We can touch a client only after we understand his or her emotional quotient [EQ]—each person's wants, needs, dreams, fears, expectations, reality, fantasy, tolerance for risk. These and other emotions all churn in unique ways within each person's soul.

"Our most critical task is to understand each client's EQ first, then respond as accurately, compassionately, and creatively as we can. That response is what I mean by 'touch,' a marvelous word that holds many positive connotations. I use it in the sense of concern, of showing concern or being concerned with another human being. I also see it as 'light,' as in 'light touch,' or the absence of heavy-handed dogma, an idea that I'll expand on later. Perhaps Shakespeare had it right when, in his play *Troilus and Cressida*, he used 'touch' to mean an expression of human feeling with which others can empathize.

"Obviously, touch is fundamental to the input and output sides of articulation. Also fundamental to the output side is writing, which is often a prerequisite for speaking. Writing is fundamental because it forces me to cleanse my thinking, to organize, expand, and prioritize my ideas, examine my logic and clarity in conveying it. That's why I find writing to be such hard work!

"Worthwhile hard work, to be sure. Work that pays off with a broader and deeper understanding that flows two ways: we understand the client, and the client understands us and knows for sure that we understand him or her. I want to take the idea of understanding to what I see as the deeper idea of 'empathy,' which I think of as getting into each other's minds, or, as the dictionaries say, 'of identifying with and fully comprehending each other.'

"I think of this mutual empathy as the essence of articulation in my business, and the reason we can touch our clients."

"What you're describing to me is the one-on-one nature of your business. Am I right?"

"I'm fortunate to enjoy the luxury of one-on-one relationships with clients, of being able to select individuals and couples with whom I want to work, and, equally important, who want to work with me. Most of them are in the top 2 percent of our population in terms of income and assets, and they're articulate as well. That simple correlation supports the thesis of this book quite nicely.

"I'm usually as comfortable working with couples as I am with individuals. Couples generally share the values, beliefs, wishes, and so on that make up a homogeneous EQ.

"On the other hand, I enjoy another type of luxury, that of avoiding working with committees. For example, I never want to work again for a group of trustees—there always seems to be six or more—responsible for an organization's pension plan. I've found over the years that each member of such a group tends to have his or her own agenda, and it often isn't relevant to managing investments.

"I wasn't always this fussy. Several years ago, before I knew better, I occasionally took on managing investments for a trust, and I actually discovered that listening to understand, one of my strengths and one skill that I insist my employees develop, was actually a detriment. I'd listen to, say, seven people, each with his or her personal agenda, and then try to respond to each in ways that touch. Impossible.

"Here's an example. I took the job of managing the investments held by a large pension fund for public employees. All meetings were open to the general public and the press, opening the door for any of the nine trustees, many of whom either held or were running for political office, to expound on their pet projects and pander for publicity and votes. That, of course, opened the doors to countless sidebar questions and conversations that were totally irrelevant to my assignment. In fact, I can point to instances when the sidebar clutter actually prevented me from doing my job.

"I found all this to be very bizarre, a colossal waste of my time, and certainly a long way outside my skill set and our definition of articulate. I also found myself at these meetings selling instead of understanding and advising, a strong contradiction of the basic beliefs that built my career and business that I found extremely disturbing. By selling I mean that, to keep the peace and prevent bickering and posturing, I'd recommend investments that I felt would satisfy the diverse interests of the trustees, but which may or may not have been the best vehicles for the fund. I compromised my recommendations and principles at the same time. That's way too political for me, so I resigned shortly after taking on the account. We all lost.

"Here's another anecdote along the same lines but with a slightly different twist. About 15 years ago I was managing the investments for a wealthy individual, an executive and board member at a midsize manufacturer. This individual and I became close friends, and he asked me to evaluate the organizational structure of his company. While that may appear to be outside my expertise, it really isn't when you consider that Allegheny is also into venture capital and we buy, fix, and sell companies.

"One quick look at the structure of this company and I knew there had to be a better way. I put together a plan, showed it to my friend, he loved it, and asked me to present it to the five-member board.

"Well, to cut to the chase, my well-crafted presentation was a disaster. During it, the other board members actually carried on sidebar conversations—really boorish. But I got the point: they weren't interested, even though it was obvious to everyone involved that my plan would save the company millions of dollars over several years. Then I got the point a second time when, in my naïve exuberance of never saying die, I tried to meet with each member individually. None gave me the courtesy.

"Later, I found out why. Each board member had his own loyalties, agenda, and financial adviser; no other adviser focused on the company's efficiency. They were snug and smug in their status quo.

"There's a bad-news, good-news ending to this story. The bad news is that this company was less profitable than it should have been, and is still leaking millions of dollars because of a board that wouldn't break away from its paralysis. The good news is that my friend is still my client, and I've worked with him on many projects in addition to managing his money.

"Is this a failure of articulation? In a way it is. I did not find the common ground needed to persuade a diverse group of only five people to my way of thinking and despite one strong ally. In another way it isn't a failure at all. I don't think that even the greatest articulators can open minds that are so tightly closed. So I'm left with a question: was the failure my inability to craft a message that touched everyone in the group, or their inability to hear, listen, and understand?

"I'm reminded of the story John Yasinsky, in Chapter 4, told about Pete Peterson's futile attempts to alert President Nixon and other top government officials to the coming energy crisis. Nobody wanted to hear it, and the country suffered greatly through the oil embargoes of the seventies. We're still suffering, in fact."

"Can you describe the steps toward your current feelings about articulation?"

"The headline answer to that question is that I went from telling people how to live their lives, to recommending strongly, and finally to influencing through gentle suggestion and letting them decide what to do. That's a complete evolution from sledgehammer to tack hammer to kid glove that I can explain further.

"I started my career as a Catholic priest. As is the case with all good priests, I was restricted in my dealings with my parishioners—I now think of them as my first clients—by the church's dogma. The church has a pretty pat solution to everybody's EQ that the parishioner either accepts or feels the consequences, a kind of do-it-or-else ultimatum. Empathy? Sure, in the form of solace and sympathy on my part, a long way from mutual understanding in the sense that parishioners knew much or anything about me.

"I would have been a better priest if I had understood the basics of articulation at the time. Judging by the bored and distracted looks on the faces of my parishioners, my sermons were flat and uninspiring and, not surprisingly, ignored. The reasons: I was growing more and more disenchanted with the church, and it showed in my halting voice and hesitant demeanor. And I didn't spend the time needed to craft a concise and uplifting message. In fact, I started to think about my sermon a half hour or so before giving it, then scribbled a few notes and strode to the podium. Today, I would start to craft my message days in advance, either outline it in detail or write it out to be sure it made sense, and present it with enthusiasm and confidence.

"I disliked being the sledgehammer of human relations and an inarticulate priest so intently that they were two of several reasons—many of the others are also related to my growing distaste and distrust of dogma—I left the church for private life.

"I then went to work as a therapist for a mental health/mental retardation agency, beginning my career as a tack hammer. Instead of telling people what to do, I helped them become aware of what they were doing and why, then let them decide if they wanted to continue or change their behavior. My clients, now a diverse group of disturbed and unhappy folks, evaluated for themselves the merits of my recommendations and could either follow them or not.

"Counseling was another good-news, bad-news story. On the good side, it added a great deal of individuality and leeway to my dealings with people, and it stretched my interpersonal skills. On the bad side, it stretched my abilities to live on a pittance, delaying my marrying and starting a family. So I looked around for a business that demanded and rewarded articulation, my growing interest in finance, and my natural inclination to help people live better lives. Financial planning fit the bill.

"In the mid-seventies I teamed up with a partner who thinks as I do. We formed Allegheny Financial, and my evolution as an Articulate slid quietly into the kid-glove stage, all of which begs for some explanation. I provide information to clients, whether during our first or fiftieth meeting, without any pressure to decide anything quickly, and especially while I'm in the room. This practice goes back to the personal nature of money that we've already discussed. Even though my clients bare their financial lives to me as much as to anyone, I still don't need to witness or be part of their decision-making process. And I always follow the principle that being uncomfortable about a decision is reason enough to do nothing; further explanation isn't needed, and asking for it is counterproductive and discomforting in itself.

"A second way to look at 'kid glove' complements the first. I try to gently sway clients to my point of view by presenting evidence needed for them to arrive at their own conclusions, and selecting words that are totally nonthreatening. When talking or writing to them, I tend to use such wording as 'Conditions in the markets are such that I think it's advisable to . . .' On the other hand, I avoid such prejudicial and heavy-handed words as 'I strongly recommend . . .' There's a big difference that clients can feel.

"My style evolved in yet another fundamental way. During my early years in financial planning, I would meet a prospect for the first time and make a generic—one size fits all—presentation on the planning process and its merits. Only one in five of my prospects elected to move on to the next step and become clients, a woefully low hit rate in this business.

"Now I ask questions for, say, 45 minutes to develop a profile of the prospect's needs and wants, his or her EQ. Only then can I tailor a presentation that is meaningful. My hit rate has jumped to four of five, solid evidence that knowing the audience is key to articulation and persuasion.

"Asking the right questions is, of course, fundamental, and the prospect's answer to one question leads inevitably to the next. I 'follow the dots' as the dots reveal themselves.

"In contrast, not asking the right questions can be counterproductive, which I can best illustrate by telling a story on myself. Our firm recently invested in land on which a large energy company had drilled one gas well and planned others within six months. Seven months later I hadn't heard anything about the new well and called to ask what was going on. I was told that the paperwork for the well was still being processed. I called several times in ensuing months and got the same answer. Finally, I called and asked about the specific well that I had in mind, not just any well on the property. I was greeted with, 'Oh, that well! It was drilled months ago and is producing nicely.' To this day I wonder why I wasn't more specific and why the person on the other end of the line didn't think to give me the whole story about the property. We both lost productive time.

"Our growth demonstrates the effectiveness of the kid glove. Today, 30 years from the date of our founding, Allegheny Financial is managed by 5 partners and employs almost 200 planners, analysts, brokers, and support personnel."

"Does articulation play a major role in hiring and retaining employees?"

"Articulation is high on the list of skills needed to work here, right up there with skills in employees' main disciplines. Perhaps articulation is the make-or-break skill when we're interviewing a candidate for an open job. For example, I won't hire anyone who isn't concise, who doesn't know when to quit talking or writing, and I won't hire anyone who can't listen.

"Running off at the mouth or keyboard is absolutely unacceptable here. And we never knowingly hire somebody who interrupts another person's sentence, or who talks over another person, or who carries on a sidebar conversation during a meeting. These personality traits are extremely boorish; they're sure to turn off clients, and they absolutely prevent us from understanding a client's EQ and to respond in ways that touch. In short, they are totally contrary to our principles.

"Not long ago we were looking outside the company for a CEO to manage the day-to-day details of the business. The partners would rather work with clients. One candidate who looked great on paper and who passed muster in preliminary interviews let his guard down at a dinner meeting with all the partners. He showed that he was addicted to management dogma, that he wasn't flexible, which of course goes against our basic principles. He also brought back all sorts of bad memories of my years with the church. He didn't get the job."

"What kinds of clients are attracted to your kid-glove approach?"

"'Financially conservative,' 'independent,' and 'concerned' are all characteristics of most of our clients. Conservative in the sense that they live below their incomes, independent in the sense that all have made their own informed decisions for many years and have been successful because of them, and concerned because many remember the Depression and fear running out of money before they pass on. The kid-glove approach appeals to all of those personality traits, which I recognize are somewhat conflicting and contradictory. One client, for example, tells me that I don't manage his money, I manage his comfort. A successful entrepreneur, he is particularly insecure and anxious about running out of money before he runs out of time, so he lives far below his means and ignores my suggestions to spend more on the simple pleasures of life. He isn't unusual. By the way, he has referred one of his sons and several of his friends to me, and they, too, fit the profile."

"What are the bottom lines here?"

"The need for articulation in everything we do permeates our company. We hire and go to great lengths to keep people who hear, listen, understand . . . then respond in ways that touch. I hope that I am a good role model for that sequence, a sequence that I think of as the very heart of articulation and our continuing success. And we go to great lengths to attract clients who appreciate our low-key brand of articulation and management style. Our growth indicates that it works for us and our clients."

6

Praising and Dissing the Articulates and the Also-Rans We've Known

Three keen observers and critics get down and dirty.

Armed to the tongue with more than 105 years of varied experiences in articulation and its lack, we felt the hubris of high qualifications to launch into our subject: this book, and the businesspeople and others we've known over the years who prove and disprove its premise.

"We" are three credible veterans of the business to help businesses communicate, albeit in different ways. Alan, a graphic designer, retired a few years ago largely because he found himself dreading another project with managers he indelicately calls "inarticulate idiots." "How many times should I be insulted by people who look at my designs and say, 'It's not quite what I had in mind,' and then, when I ask gently for just a tad of specifics, I'm told, 'I don't know; it's just not right.' Now, I don't mind people not liking my work; I've been around long enough to know that I can't please everyone all the time. But that kind of circular abstraction borders on musing of the most superficial sort, and it's surely not being helpful or articulate. I chose not to work with those kinds of people."

Kevin has been employed as a middle manager by several firms during his career and is now a rung or two from the top at a high-tech company that specializes in imaging and document control. "I've worked with bosses who are both articulate and not, and I gotta tell you that articulate is better and easier because I know where I stand and where

50

andRe I'm going. Working with an inarticulate boss is like winking at a woman at the opposite end of a dark bar: I know what I'm doing, I'm not at all sure it's the right thing to do, and nobody else knows or cares I'm there."

The last member of our little focus group is me, your author, a scribe, since 1970, of more than three million words of what I fondly call "corporate gargle." You, friendly reader, can imagine the parade of managers I've worked with and their wide range of articulation and its lack. Why, I remember . . .

"Whoa," said Alan. "I want to start with the good news and talk about Dave Green at PPG Industries, an Articulate in an unusual way. Dave was the ultimate pacifier with words. He never offended, yet he was always candid—is it possible to be candid in business and not offend? He was sincere. Yet, despite his soft tone—or was it because of?—he always got his point across. Everyone he communicated with knew where he stood on any issue, and I think that skill was one reason he rose to vice president of advertising and public relations."

"I wrote a series of articles for a marketing manager at PPG and ran into Dave soon after they were published in an internal magazine," I interjected. "I asked him how he liked them. He told me that the writing was great, but the typography 'needed help.' I read the final piece and saw what he meant; there were typos and other blips all over the place. He could have been much harsher than that euphemism 'needed help'; he could have said the typography really sucks. Nevertheless, I got the message loud and clear."

Kevin added: "Dave reminds me of the president of a small company I worked with about five years ago. I'll call him Alf. This guy was great in crowds; he could work a room and take over, and his speeches were always what I call 'on point' or 'on message.' By that I mean that his message was always germane to the audience, and he never wasted or shouted a word.

"I remember his talk to a group of stock analysts and bankers when he took the company public. He explained his vision clearly, succinctly, quickly, so that everyone in the room knew exactly where he was leading the business, and why. That's articulate: taking a complex subject and boiling it down to its simpler core."

"Let's talk about that skill, to boil down the complex to the simple," I said. "John Yasinsky took years to develop it, and then he observed and studied it among the power brokers while at the White House for a year. That experience changed his career path and his life. On the opposite side of the coin, I think that the person who displayed that skill the least in recent memory was Al Gore during the 2000 election campaign. When he was nominated in August that year, I bet several people the best dinner in Pittsburgh that he would win by at least 100 electoral votes. I reasoned that people vote their pocketbooks, and Gore, as vice president in the two Clinton administrations, had been a visible part of the biggest economic boom and expansion in history.

"I'm convinced that I lost those bets, and Gore lost the election, at least in part because Gore couldn't, or wouldn't, find a way to attach himself to the boom times and distance himself from the Clinton scandals at the same time. That's a complex mixture of goods and bads that, if he had found a way to communicate it, might have changed the course of human events.

"A friend asked me recently: if articulation is so important to rising to the top, why did Bush Two become president despite being inarticulate to the point where many people joke about it? Forgetting about the election snafus, my answer is that, yes, Bush is inarticulate, but Gore is more so. There are rungs on the ladder of articulation and inarticulation, and you can look good or bad depending on the differential between the rungs on which the sender and receiver are standing.

"I want to go back to Kevin's idea of being 'on point.' I think Gore was 'off point'; he missed the point that full wallets mean votes, and my wallet became significantly thinner because of it. And, as Georgia Berner points out in Chapter 9, Bush's message somehow resonated with a wide swath of voters. She couldn't explain what she means by 'somehow resonated.'

"I have another example of being off point. A number of years ago I was commissioned to write a long article based on a two-hour speech by John Marous. At the time, John was vice president, international, for Westinghouse, and he had been trained at various charm schools to change his articulation skills from downright ungrammatical and 'Pittsburghese' to 'smooth talker.' He was to explain to some 2000 employees how Westinghouse would expand its business overseas and how that expansion would benefit the company and every employee.

"I tried to take notes for my article and found that I couldn't, simply because I couldn't find any meat. All I found was a ceaseless babble of pointless verbosity. The real message streaming from this man was that there is no message at all, unless, of course, you think of bluster as message.

"Right after the speech, several friends and I adjourned to the nearest pub to discuss what we had heard. They—my friends—were enthused with the whole experience: a great presentation, smooth, well done, well organized and orchestrated, and so on. I listened to them chat for a while before asking a few basic questions: What main point or points did he make? What solid ideas for new business did you come away with? What did he say that would change the way you do business?

"Blank stares, open mouths, the silence of ice clinking against glass. The fact is that John had said nothing in 15,000 words, but he had said it with pinache and verve. He had given us thin gruel when we were looking for thick steak.

"My problem was writing a 2000-word article based on air, and I explained that to my client, the director of communications for the entire corporation. He didn't believe me, of course, so we went to the considerable expense of transcribing the entire tape of the presentation so he could read it. [Careful reading, like careful writing, can uncover all sorts of logic and other fallacies of thinking, as any careful reader understands.]

"After reading the transcript, my client agreed with me that substance wasn't John's strong suit. As an aside, he was subsequently chairman of the company and was instrumental in its demise, which is another subject for another book."

Kevin asked, "Did you find a way to write the article?"

I chuckled, "I wrote it based on what John should or could have said, then I gave the draft to John for his review and approval before publication. He then rose to new levels of self-delusion and congratulated me for a job well done. 'Great article. You synthesized exactly what I said. Print it.' We did.

"Which leads me to another related point: articulate people often save the careers of Also-Rans, but only if the Also-Rans know they need help."

"If they're Also-Rans, how did they get to the top slots in the organization?" Alan asked. "Doesn't that contradict the basic premise of the book?"

Kevin replied, "Not always. It depends on the needs of the company, which, as we all know, can change quite rapidly. I have a great example.

"Alf, who I talked about a few minutes ago, was a fine articulator and manager of people; he knew how to build the team of engineers and scientists needed to develop and refine the company's products. He didn't know how to do that himself, and the company grew rapidly during its early years.

"Then the entire industry went through some extreme rumblings called technological change. Suddenly, research and product development—all the phases of engineering with a touch of pure science—became top priority.

"Alf appointed a brilliant engineer to the presidency. This man was so brilliant that he knew he was marginally articulate and didn't want to be more adept. So he surrounded himself with engineers and others who were truly part of that group we call the Articulates, and he handed the responsibility for most internal and external communications to them. He didn't lock himself away entirely, mind you, but he was far less visible than Alf. It worked."

Alan responded, "Monte Wilkinson did the same thing. A manager of communications at PPG, Monte was the zenith of an Also-Ran—glaringly inept on both the input and output sides of articulation. Nevertheless, he survived in the corporate world for 20 or more years by surrounding himself with people who he paid, with PPG's money, to be his surrogate Articulates.

"Monte was educated at the very best universities, where he majored in communications. Somehow, his education didn't take. For example, he never learned to listen and process information; having a conversation with him was like talking to yourself, akin to the political debates. Question: What does the marketing manager want to say about this product? Answer: Can we have another drink now?

"But, like Alf's successor, Monte was smart enough to know that he either couldn't or wouldn't communicate. I suspect wouldn't, because he always struck me as extremely lazy. So he surrounded himself with really good writers, designers, and creative thinkers who took the load of articulation off his back and mind. Ironically, PPG realized, after at least two decades of this covert and expensive chicanery, that Monte, whose job it was to communicate the company's story but couldn't, was farming out his job to a bunch of high-priced practitioners who could. He was fired and now, a few years later, he's still unemployed. His lack of articulation caught up with him at PPG and spread throughout the entire communications business in this small town."

THE ORIGIN OF SPECIOUS

"I think that the pinnacle of inarticulation is the typical business meeting," said Alan. "Every 3-hour meeting I've attended could have been 15 minutes, or not taken place at all, if only the attendees had focused on the topic and been prepared to discuss it."

"I agree," I chortled. "Most meetings are whirlpools of absurdities; they are plagued with all sorts of bad habits that actually destroy articulation, particularly on the input side. Attendees hold sidebar conversations, talk over each other, interrupt willy-nilly—all the bad habits that literally prevent listening and understanding. Jim Browne would never put up with that.

"Just think of what those bad habits do to destroy productivity. Not long ago I was at a meeting of 15 IT managers when it came to a screeching halt when one attendee offered the latest rumor about an affair the president was supposedly carrying on with a rather comely vice president on his staff. Suddenly, everyone at the meeting chimed in with his or her take, and a business meeting turned into a gossip-fest for at least an hour."

• • • •

I was lunching with a friend who runs a small engineering company, Ken Lovorn, and we were discussing this book. "The premise is right on," he said, "and I have a story to prove it. We advertised for a receptionist and interviewed four of the respondents, all of whom looked good on paper. One spoke ungrammatical English—I swear that she couldn't match a noun to a verb if her life depended on it. Another was addicted to what we call 'Pittsburghese' with all the 'yunzes' and other colloquialisms that turn off articulate people everywhere. The third couldn't stop talking, and we don't need constant chatter in our offices. [Jim Browne agrees; he won't hire a person who doesn't know when to stop talking.]

"The fourth applicant fit the job perfectly. She was educated to be a receptionist at a fine secretarial school, wants to be the best receptionist ever, and is totally aware that standard English is key. We're looking forward to a long and satisfying relationship."

Joe D, profiled in Chapter 8, noted that we laugh at lawyers for their convoluted language and then call on them to be our communicators. "Why?" he asks rhetorically. "Because we trust them to say whatever's needed to keep us out of legal trouble. My wife recently asked our lawyer to write a simple letter about a simple matter, although she is perfectly capable of writing it. Just another case of lawyers taking over what we can do ourselves."

I told my own lawyer story. "While in the midst of my divorce, I asked my lawyer to write a letter to my wife and her lawyer about a simple matter in our settlement. He did, and it was full of the heretos, whatfors, and parties of the first part that are endemic in legalese. I wrote the letter in language my wife could understand and faxed it to my lawyer for approval. 'You can't send that!' he shouted over the phone, 'she'll understand it!' 'Just what I want,' I replied, and off it went. My lawyer didn't know that he had given me a wonderful compliment.

"And Rob Bucenell, a former communications and HR manager at PPG Industries, told me of a brilliant chemist at one of PPG's plants who literally couldn't or wouldn't talk about his accomplishments, so other people took credit for his work and were promoted over him. Everyone at his level knew that he was key to the plant's efficiency and the success of its products; upper management, however, didn't have a clue. So he was stuck in a midlevel position throughout his 30-year career. I find it hard to believe that he liked it there, but . . .

"I also understand that few people can tell the difference between honest and subtle praise about their accomplishments and blatant self-promotion, so they clam up. My advice to them is to find ways to softly slide their accomplishments into other conversations; don't address them directly. Offhand remarks can be very convincing, or, as marketing gurus will tell you, a whisper is more persuasive than a shout. It's all part of being articulate, and everyone will get the point."

7

Sherry
Davis Guth

*From Ms. Chitty-Chat Middle Manager
to Ms. On-Point Senior Staff.*

"Marketing is my passion," says Sherry Davis Guth, senior director of marketing and communications for TelCove, the leading provider of premium telecommunications services to businesses along the eastern seaboard. "And effective marketing literally and explicitly demands the highest levels of articulation to our internal and external audiences." Musing, she continues her string of thoughts: "Of course, marketing blankets every function of our company, so I'm not stretching a point by saying that TelCove is a company that thinks of articulation as its heart and soul.

"Which we should. TelCove is in the business of helping other businesses communicate through a variety of Internet, data, and voice services. We transport our services via one of the most secure and reliable fiber optic networks in the industry. We're in the hardware side of articulation, the equipment and technology through which communication is sent, and it's obviously very important.

"I didn't consciously realize or understand the importance of articulation during the first several years of my career, but I sure do now. I spent the first 2 years of my business life in human resources, then moved to product management, marketing, and business management—a total of 20 years in the telecommunications industry, the last 8 with TelCove.

"Early in my career my peers dubbed me Ms. Chitty-Chat, and, I'm sorry and reluctant to admit, the name fit me like a glove. Seems I never quit yakking away on any old subject. I even subjected customers to what I would now define as irrelevant blathering. I was, in fact, off point a good part of the time. I spoke too often and thought too late. Backwards habit #1.

"Worse yet, I was impatient and too quick to make decisions. I often wonder how many bad or marginal decisions I made and if my chitty-chat nature was the root cause. I was a good example of the management style that we now define as Fire, Aim, Ready. Backwards habit #2.

"During that period of my life I suppose I would be part of the inarticulate Also-Rans. Perhaps I was showing off my extended vocabulary and quick mind with my glibness, which is exactly what Articulates avoid."

THE TURNING POINT AND THE FIRST STEPS TOWARD ARTICULATION

"Then, about a dozen years into my career, while working as a senior product manager at TelCove, and with a new master of science degree in marketing, I was offered a promotion to a regional marketing manager, which required daily interaction with a regional vice president of sales. Since there were two positions open at the time, I had to choose which VP I wanted to work with.

"And here is a subtale of Also-Rans versus Articulates. One VP—I'll call him Mr. Pinehurst—was a blustery, good-old-boy extrovert right out of the old school of selling, which some people think of as articulate, but really isn't. A pat on the back, hearty laugh, a golf game, and he figured the sale was his. We were like oil and water except for two unfortunate traits: we were both too verbose and too quick to make decisions, a mixture for a bad cocktail.

"The other VP, Bob, couldn't be more opposite—thoughtful, patient, insightful, and articulate in the sense that he thought for as long as he needed before he spoke or wrote. Not surprisingly, his messages were always concise and on point. At first, he drove me crazy with his patience, then he drove me sane with his abilities to think rationally and arrive at the right decisions. I came to realize that, like other Articulates, he could connect a wide range of diverse ideas and draw conclusions that weren't at all obvious to we impatient ones.

"Before I made my decision, I watched how each behaved in meetings. Mr. Pinehurst would sit at the most visible spot and take over with his bluster; Bob would sit unobtrusively aside and remain quiet until he had something important to say, and then he'd drop the most insightful pearls of wisdom on the group, leaving them in awe.

"I like to think of myself as pretty cerebral, and I saw that trait in Bob. Sensing that very important compatibility, I went to work supporting him and his region, and it turned out to be the best decision I've ever made in my career. To jump to the bottom line, after working with an Articulate for only two years, I too became a true Articulate. That led to another promotion to my current position of senior director of marketing and communications. More importantly, however, Bob was deservedly promoted to CEO and president. Mr. Pinehurst, well, he decided to leave TelCove to start his own company that competed directly with TelCove. Two years later, Mr. Pinehurst's company filed for Chapter 7 and he tried to be rehired by TelCove, but by then our culture had changed dramatically—I'll get into that in a minute—and we didn't have any reason or need for a glad-hander."

THE PRE-BOB ERA

"Before 2002, TelCove was known as Adelphia Business Solutions [ABS], a wholly owned subsidiary of Adelphia Communications, a public, family-controlled company that owned and operated cable television networks. The patriarch of the controlling family, John Rigas, appointed one of his three sons to be CEO of ABS, a position he held from the late nineties through 2002, sparking an age of inarticulation. Extremely bright, the CEO was also very shy and somewhat uncomfortable in front of an audience.

"The first casualty of this culture of reticence during that time was marketing. It was reduced to such trinkets as coffee mugs and golf balls printed with the company's logo. Press releases, speeches to employees and customers, and general interaction with the media took place so infrequently that they were unnoticed and ineffective.

"The second casualty was the company's culture and efficiency. We essentially didn't have a culture simply because we didn't communicate constructively. Employees, via a survey completed after I moved to our corporate offices, clearly revealed that they thought the company was mismanaged and rudderless, and top managers couldn't be trusted to act in the best interests of the company and its employees and customers. Many also said, quite candidly, that, if offered, they would accept a position at another firm. Not surprising, morale was at an all-time low, and productivity had hit the skids as employees, I suspect, spent more time griping and looking for other employment opportunities than they did working.

"I showed the results of the survey to our shy CEO, suggested that open communications from the top could help to solve the problems, and recommended various programs that would explain his strategies and goals for the company. For example, I recommended brown-bag lunches with employees to answer questions and share ideas, figuring that the conversational informality of such events would get him over his shyness and discomfort. Not so; he rejected the idea and, unfortunately, most of the others.

"In January 2002, Adelphia spun off ABS as a separate company. A few months later, ABS filed for bankruptcy, in part because of the inefficiencies created by management, and in part because of the general downturn of the industry. These two causes are, of course, related: an inefficient company is less able to weather a downturn than an efficient one.

"Additionally, and during the same time frame, Adelphia Communications filed for bankruptcy, and in May 2002 the Rigas scandal made the headlines of the business press from the *Wall Street Journal* to the local papers in the town in which Adelphia was headquartered. As a result, ABS's CEO, who is a Rigas, chose to resign and was replaced in June 2002 by Bob, who by that time had established himself as the heir apparent.

"The post-Bob era kicked off in typical Bob fashion and with a single goal: to manage the company out of bankruptcy and into profitability. That single focus was complicated greatly by the Adelphia scandal, low employee morale, and even lower productivity. He and his staff faced a multiple whammy of the worst kind.

"Bob began the task the way you'd expect from a man with his level of patience. He studied the situation carefully and thoroughly, and called on his staff for advice and counsel. He and I discussed and analyzed the current state of the company, then we developed a survival plan that was based on his talents for articulation. Key to the plan was open, honest, two-way communications that would utilize all available media and build respect and trust with employees and customers.

"Working intently with Bob to develop and implement the survival and communications plans transformed me into a better Articulate. For example, he insisted on the 'Three Bullet Rule': any message worth communicating can be done in three bullets. That's hard work, really hard, but it literally forces me to extract the essence of my message before I send it. He taught me to think before talking or writing, to engage my mind before I engaged my mouth or keyboard. Quite a turnaround for Ms. Chitty-Chat!"

HAS ARTICULATION WORKED?

"Let's look at the record and you decide. TelCove emerged from bankruptcy in April 2004, only two years after filing. Perhaps the magnitude of the achievement is clearer when considering that only 1 in 10 companies that file for bankruptcy successfully emerges, much less experiences profitable growth. Which we certainly did. Today, TelCove is a $315 million company, employs 1400 people, has a presence in 70 U.S. markets, and serves 14,000 customers. I think that that's an impressive turnaround, as does our board.

"During the restructuring process, we kept the visionaries and Articulates on the payroll, and parted ways with the Also-Rans—raising productivity and morale. Our existing customers value us—losing one is rare—and new customers choose us regularly so we're experiencing and enjoying significant sales growth.

"The key? Open, honest communication that builds respect and trust both internally and externally—that's our definition of articulation, and it's worked for us. I can't imagine why it wouldn't work for every business."

8

Joe D

Meet an engineer/executive who knows the value of articulation and practices it to the hilt.

"My abilities to articulate have been major factors behind my success in the engineering business simply because they overcome my deficiencies as an engineer. I suppose that I could design a beam if I had a gun to my head, for example, but I'm so inept and slow that I couldn't make much of a living at designing it or anything else. However, I can convince clients that a beam is needed and convince civil engineers that they should design it. I suppose that's salesmanship and delegation; it's also articulation."

Joe D, PhD, PE (professional engineer), is director of environmental engineering for one of the world's largest engineering firms. Dr. D is an outspoken advocate of articulation as a route to the success of individuals and organizations, and a vociferous critic of an education system that either glosses over or ignores the language and its pivotal role in thinking and decision making. For example, most graduates of engineering schools, with whom he is most familiar, "cannot string two sentences together that make sense, and, more the pity, don't recognize that they can't and don't know why they should."

Joe and I were lunching in Pittsburgh to discuss this book.

"Joe, engineers are typically laughed at for their clumsiness with the language."

"Most should be, for two reasons. First, they don't understand that the two most important products of the engineering business are proposals and reports, whether they are written or spoken. Both are deliverables that reflect engineering intelligence, of course—intelligence that can't be conveyed without articulation. Second, they haven't taken a class or opened a book on writing or speaking since high school, if then. So they have no reason to think that articulation is important.

"I feel sorry for an engineer—anyone, really—who just doesn't 'get' those simple facts of business life. On the other hand, I understand why they don't: nobody told them, not their professors in college or their bosses. On still another hand, I can't afford to hire engineers who don't display some sensitivity to the language—they can really throw productivity into a cocked hat and destroy, with one insensitive document, relationships with customers that took years to build. Finding engineers who are sensitive to language narrows my choices greatly—I'd say by 90 percent or more. Yeah, I'd guess that only 1 in 10 engineers gets it."

"Can you tell me about a few engineers who do 'get it'?"

"Here's one of my few happy experiences. About eight years ago I was at a trade meeting and was impressed by the comments of a young man that were particularly insightful, concise, and coherent. I made it a point to introduce myself to him and exchange business cards. About two years later I needed an engineer, resurrected this man's card, called him, and offered him the job. Now, six years later, he is surely my most valued and valuable employee.

"Not only is he an accomplished engineer, he is the only person in my group, other than me, who displays his articulation by writing articles for trade publications and making presentations at conventions and seminars. He and I occasionally coauthor papers. In addition, he is the only person in my group who I trust to communicate to customers without my first editing his text. The bottom line is that he understands the value of articulation in terms of publicity for himself and our firm. He actually increases my productivity and the productivity of our group.

"One of our project engineers is another plus. When I first hired him I wasn't too concerned about his writing; I was more focused on completing a very complex engineering assignment. Later, though, he had to write reports to customers. They were, to be polite, nonsense. The man didn't understand what he was saying, and he didn't know a comma from a period.

"I explained to him that I respected his engineering skills but couldn't tolerate his bad writing and suggested a course or two at the local university and some books on the subject to study. He acted on my recommendation, proving that some engineers can see the light and react positively.

"His writing now isn't the greatest, but it's passable in that it's clear and understandable. Customers haven't complained, which is the acid test, and I don't need to perform major surgery on his work; a light edit is usually enough."

"Let's talk about the productivity busters, those who I call the Also-Rans. I've known a few. One is a sales engineer who is so glib, which always comes across as shallow and without substance, and verbose, which always indicates a mind so lazy that it can't find the essence of the message, that he can't hold a job for more than a year or two. He can talk himself into a job, but soon his employer discovers that he's a bit of a fraud and time waster. Customers react the same way."

"Being flowery and verbose is just another form of inarticulation, a form that I can't stomach or tolerate. Nevertheless, I know too many engineers who think that using too many words, and too many big and obscure words, is a sign of intelligence and insight, when, in fact, it is a sign of pomposity and murkiness. A few years ago I inherited an engineer from another department who regularly used words such as 'sustainability' and phrases like 'green design' and 'multipollutant.' Their meanings are so broad and they are used so widely and irresponsibly that they are meaningless. When I asked this person what he means, I was rewarded with the thousand-mile stare and 'everyone knows'—sure signs of a lazy mind.

"My graduate students reacted the same way when I asked them to define 'sustainable,' the big buzzword in the environmental business these days. One student actually scoffed: 'Everyone knows; this is silly, a waste of class time.'

"So I called on each of my seven students to define the word and got seven widely divergent answers. Then I asked them: 'How can we

communicate accurately without a shared understanding of meaning?' I
wonder if they got the point."

"Let's go back to the Also-Rans in my business. I had to fire an engineer
just last week because he is very wordy; he probably writes three times
as many words than needed to do the job. Then, he ignored my edits;
he had fallen in love with his words—a cardinal sin of writing—so he
was blind to his own failings. I've run across other engineers who write
what I call 'kaleidoscope krud,' a morass of words in random patterns
that may be pretty but are meaningless because the colors and shapes—
thoughts—aren't connected, indicating mental chaos that is all too common. And a temporary receptionist drove me nuts by misspelling even
simple words.

"I try to avoid those kinds of problems by always asking potential
employees for a sample of their best writing before I hire them, which
can either stop me from hiring the wrong person or point me to the right
person. One applicant sent me a few pages of a report that were just
awful; I had no idea what he was trying to say. When I pointed this out
to him, he chuckled and said that he didn't like the piece either and it
wasn't his best work.

"'So why did you send it to me?' I asked, a bit dumbfounded.
'Because it was handy, and I figured that I should respond as soon as
possible.' I didn't offer him a job. Can you imagine how that attitude
would destroy our relationships with clients? I can hear him telling clients: 'Yeah, I know the report is lousy, but I didn't have time [that is, "I
was too lazy or didn't plan my tasks"] to write it well.'"

"I tell my students 'better late than wrong' with their assignments. And
when one apologizes for bad writing when handing in a paper, I hand it
back and ask why I should waste my time reading junk.

"A local real estate developer needs to get that message. Not long
ago he e-mailed me the first five pages of a proposal, asked me to review
them, and invited me to lunch at his posh club for a chat. When I pointed
out the many egregious structural and grammatical errors in just those
few pages, he said he wasn't surprised: he had banged out this draft at
two o'clock in the morning and wasn't 'with it.' I showed great restraint
by not leaping across the table that separated us and strangling him.

"Joe, you said that your abilities to articulate are key to your career
and implied that without those abilities you couldn't make as good a

living in the engineering profession as you can with them. What's the history here?"

"I first became aware of the importance of articulation in a Jesuit high school. A teacher there assigned a short essay every week—it was due every Monday morning—and one misspelling or grammatical error of any type attracted the teacher's wrath and a failing grade. I hated that class and teacher. But when I look back, I realize how valuable that class was; I learned the importance of taking care of the details, so much so that I cringe when I see all the sloppy writing with which we're all bombarded.

"I was called on constantly to write proposals and to speak on the radio when I was a mere lad of 25 working for the environmental health group of the county health department. At the time, radio talk shows and prerecording were pretty new, and most people feared being interviewed live, but I was too naïve to be afraid. So I became the designated spokesman for a variety of environmental issues. That experience forced me to analyze my audience and purpose more carefully and accurately, become a quick study, and learn to condense my messages to what the audience needs to know—no more, no less.

"I then moved to Drexel University in Philadelphia on a full, two-year graduate fellowship awarded primarily on a detailed application/ proposal that I'm sure was evaluated as much for readability as it was for raw content. While there, I simultaneously authored a master's thesis in business administration and a doctoral dissertation in environmental engineering; both were subsequently published.

"I then moved to the National Center for Resource Recovery in Washington, DC, where I rubbed elbows and minds with dozens of very bright and articulate people. Most had published articles in juried magazines; some had written books; many were asked to speak at trade meetings and in front of Congress and congressional committees. They all seemed much smarter than me, more comfortable with their subjects, and much more accustomed to having their words actually read by people in power. It was my first experience with big-time writers/researchers—people whose articles and books I had been reading for years and respected. I was intimidated, and, at the same time, I knew that to hold my own with these heavy hitters I had to examine my own writing and improve it quickly. Recognizing the high standards of my peers and that there was actually an international audience for my writing were strong motivators.

"Watching these heavy hitters in action reinforced my already-strong ideas about the powers of articulation to influence the direction of careers and organizations. I discovered that being articulate allows me—anyone, really—to introduce my thinking to a much wider audience. It elevates Articulates to a higher plane of intelligence and creates the impression of authority even if it is self-appointed. It does all this even if their technical skills are no better, or perhaps worse, than those who are less articulate—those unknown toilers who hide their talents under a basket. Which reminds me of a passage from the Book of Matthew in the Bible: 'Neither do men light a candle, and put it under a bushel, but on a candlestick, and it giveth light to all that are in the house. Let your light shine before men, that they may see your good works.'

"With these insights in mind, I honed my skills and wrote articles, spoke to environmental and other groups, was elected president of several professional societies, and sat on boards and committees of a number of trade associations. My abilities to articulate were, and still are, called into play when documenting consensus or disagreement among group members and when writing summaries of meetings and recommendations for further actions. I'm sure that this exposure and experience were instrumental in my return to Pittsburgh to head an environmental engineering company, where I repeatedly applied my newly honed skills at articulation.

"I'm still in demand for these tasks mainly because I'm articulate, and, as corollaries, I make decisions that get things done, and I know how and when to compromise. As a result, I'm well known and respected in the engineering and consulting business, which, of course, attracts requests for proposals, lowering our sales costs. Has it led to additional business? I don't know for sure, but I'd bet it has. Has it opened new doors for my personal advancement? Absolutely.

"I really feel sorry for engineers and others who don't see those simple connections."

9
Georgia Berner

This president of a fast-growing manufacturer and aspiring U.S. congresswoman places a high value on articulation.

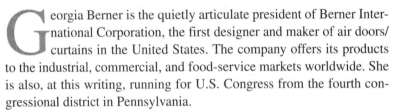

Georgia Berner is the quietly articulate president of Berner International Corporation, the first designer and maker of air doors/curtains in the United States. The company offers its products to the industrial, commercial, and food-service markets worldwide. She is also, at this writing, running for U.S. Congress from the fourth congressional district in Pennsylvania.

I first met Georgia at her modest office, which she says is "too big for my image" and is cluttered with piles of papers of the busy manager and photos of the family of the busy mother. Georgia has been named one of the top 10 bosses in the United States by *Fortune Small Business* magazine. She has also been named "Entrepreneur of the Year" and her company "Pennsylvania's Top Manufacturer" and "Best Place to Work" by various business and civic associations. I met her later in her even more modest campaign headquarters in a small town in the center of her district. Georgia and I discussed her career and her feelings toward articulation.

"I'm a synthesizer, a strong believer and unrelenting practitioner of listening to employees, customers, constituents, and the world, then organizing what I read and hear. My best talent is to make sense out of myriad facts, figures, and opinions that I gather by listening and reading, then distilling them to information that's useful—meaningful—to my business and personal lives. Today, especially since 9/11, that's called 'connecting the dots,' and it places me solidly on the input side of

CLOWT. It also places me in the best possible position to move to the output side—to write and speak in ways that persuade firmly, politely, and quietly, and to test the effectiveness of the message.

"Articulation has been a major influence in my career, which I can demonstrate with a bit of history and a few anecdotes. My late husband, Christian, began working at Berner International in 1972. I was peripherally involved—it wasn't my full-time passion—in the business at the time; I say peripherally because I was also raising two sons and two daughters and running our household. Nevertheless, my husband told me often that I understood business in general and this business in particular as well as anyone, and therefore I could manage it as well as anyone.

"After his death in a plane crash in 1984, his confidence in me was put to the reality test: I became president of the firm. And here I am, 22 years later, still in the corner office—if mostly in spirit since I decided to run for public office and relinquished day-to-day operations. You might say that I've reverted to being peripherally involved in managing a company that has grown sixfold since I took over, and is getting ready to celebrate its fiftieth anniversary. We're a good, responsible corporate citizen by offering outstanding products at competitive prices to customers, and steady work that pays well to employees.

"Articulation played a big role. So big, in fact, that the heart of our mission statement is 'Berner . . . is dedicated to listening to and solving customers' problems . . .' You'll find that statement on many walls throughout our plant and offices and in almost all of our brochures and other promotional material. I want to make sure that it's never far from the eyes and minds of employees and customers.

"Listening, as you've said often, Pete, is the rarest skill in business today, and probably the rarest in our society as a whole. The reason seems clear to me: we're actually taught to *not* listen—or to listen in very short bursts, a subject that I'll get into later—by media dedicated to sound bites and talk-show hosts and their guests who constantly shout their interruptions like kids fighting over a toy. What a shame, because listening is the first step toward connecting the dots and making informed decisions.

"An example: my sales manager told me early on and in good faith that we were participating fully in the food-service business, but even a cursory review of our sales to that segment, combined with a marketing study, suggested to me that we were a minor player at best. Many potential customers in the business said that they had never heard of us!

"Synthesizing those gross contradictions could lead only to confusion and indecision; I needed more information. So I met with a major supplier of food-service equipment, who told me that he had never heard of us. He then took me to meet his design team. The few who had heard of us were very candid: they couldn't or wouldn't specify us because the electrical switch we used was too expensive (they also agreed, in something of a cognitive dissonance, that our air curtains are the best on the market). They also said that shipping by truck added to the cost without adding any benefit, and our reps—we sell through a network of manufacturers' reps—didn't specialize in the restaurant business so they didn't really understand it, and they didn't see them often or at all.

"The bottom line was that they liked our product but couldn't tolerate our total price or the way we sold to them.

"Given this new information, the dots became clear and easy to connect, leading to several decisions. First, I challenged—actually, I insisted politely and firmly—our engineers to design curtains that were competitive in price, superior in performance, and shippable by UPS. Then I contacted each of our reps, explained the situation, and gave them a year to develop food-service accounts and document the relationships. At the end of the year, we hired a food-service sales manager and began setting up a network of sales reps specifically for this market.

"In essence, we designed and built a new product line and a new network through which to sell. It's worked, and we're now well known in the business and are booking substantial sales. Would it have worked without articulation on both the input and output sides? Of course not.

"Here's a bad-news, good-news story about articulation. Back in 1984, I inherited, along with the business, a plant manager who was disagreeable, authoritarian, undiplomatic, and unresponsive to workers' needs or complaints. You get the picture. I recognized that he was failing on both sides of the articulation process.

"I first talked to him about changing his style, and I'm convinced that he didn't hear or understand a word I said, still more evidence that listening to understand is a rare skill even when that person's job is at stake. The situation became more contentious, and I eventually had to fire him. I ran the plant myself for a short time before noticing that our purchasing clerk knew the ins and outs of the process better than anyone. I offered her the job, convinced her that she could do it when she insisted that she couldn't, and helped her during the first months of transition.

"What a change! We now have a manager who is polite, diplomatic, willing to listen to employees on the floor and to learn, and a team player—everything the former manager wasn't. Employees like and respect her, surely because she likes and respects them. Funny how it always works that way! Productivity has soared, relationships with employees are far more cordial, and relationships with the union are so smooth and peaceful that our union offered us a 10-year agreement that satisfied everyone involved—practically unheard of these days.

"Opportunities to be articulate turn up in the darndest places and at the darndest times. I was in a large supermarket not long ago and noticed that our air curtain was caked with a quarter inch of grime. I tracked down the store's manager, introduced myself, and explained—again politely and directly—that the grime was lowering the efficiency of the air curtain, raising the store's ongoing costs for electricity and eventually the larger cost for replacement or major repair.

"She listened, then asked when she could expect our people to clean the unit. I explained to her how easy it was to remove the grime and suggested that she add the task to her regular maintenance schedule. She must have done that because now, when I visit the store, I check the unit and it's always squeaky clean. Will that small act lead to future business for us? Probably.

"Here's another anecdote. I was on a plane and started to chat with the man in the adjoining seat, as passengers do. Turned out he was in the restaurant business and had some air curtains made by a competitor, wasn't particularly pleased with their performance, and asked what I thought of their products. In my usual direct way, I said simply, 'They don't work well or efficiently' and went 'Argh!' while putting my finger down my throat.

"He laughed for minutes, then jokingly asked me, 'What do you *really* think?' He then agreed with me. A month or two later we had an order for replacement units.

"Here's an example with a different twist. I was invited to speak to a group of specifying engineers working for a big-box retailer. I spoke for maybe 15 minutes about the technology of how our products work before realizing that I was losing my audience. Flustered, I rushed through the remainder of my presentation, fearing that I had bungled an important sales opportunity.

"One attendee approached me after the meeting to tell me that I had given them 'more information than they needed or wanted,' a perfect definition of wordiness or lack of concision, and a perfect formula for boring listeners and readers. He explained further that the engineers at the meeting are interested in how well the units perform, how well they meet performance specifications. They are far less interested in the technology behind the performance. I learned right then and there to never assume that I know the audience's interests, and that I must research them carefully before preparing my remarks or writing a proposal.

"Which brings me to the output side of articulation. I detest obfuscation in myself and in others; I revere clarity, concision, and purposefulness in both writing and speaking. As a result, I am direct in that I try to get my point across clearly and in the fewest possible words, and I try to never offend by choosing the wrong words or being abrupt or demanding.

"I feel that those qualities are important for everybody, but particularly for women in business. I find it unfortunate—and I know I'm generalizing here—that most businessmen expect and accept those qualities in other men and fear them in women. Instead, they want the lace and sugar-coated words that never seem to get the job done."

"Georgia, does articulation enter into your decisions to either hire a new employee or retain an existing one? Has it in the past? Jim Browne, in Chapter 5, rejects interrupters and babblers, and Joe D, in Chapter 8, asks applicants to submit a sample of their best writing before he'll go to the first interview."

"We hire for fit; that is, we hire the talents that match the job and the personalities and values that match Berner's, so articulation enters into our decisions more for one job than another. Our salespeople, for example, are extremely articulate; they live our mission statement to listen to customers and solve their problems every day. Our design engineers and plant manager come in a close second. I select these people by gut instinct more than by a formal test, and it's worked well so far.

"However, I do have some built-in filters. I automatically disqualify candidates who show, with their language, that they are control freaks, schmoozers, flatterers, and runners-on, those who can't seem to stop talking. And I reject anyone, man or woman, who I sense is impatient at being interviewed by a woman. They give themselves away by giving short answers to complex questions, as if to say, 'What does a woman know about production or business?' Then there are the basics: avoiding looking me in the eye, chewing gum, too many 'you knows' and 'you sees' that indicate a lazy mind.

"We retain employees by encouraging communications. I tell people who come to me with issues to be resolved to discuss them with all the others who are involved. In the rare instances where that doesn't work, I'll sit in as facilitator. I question and probe a lot, then offer my counsel or require them to get professional counseling. Our success rate with this procedure is about 90 percent and would be higher if those who don't fit were more able to understand what doesn't work and adjust accordingly. In those cases, I suggest that they change companies.

"The bottom line is, simply, that we're pleased with our success and are aware that articulate employees play an important role in it."

"Has your thinking about articulation changed since you started your run for Congress?"

"Yes and no. Articulation is at least as important at every level of government as it is at every level of business; nothing's changed there. The requirements, however, are worlds apart; there are fundamental differences.

"Let's talk first about importance by examining the Bush-Gore and Bush-Kerry campaigns. I think Bush spoke the right words and sound bites that resonated with voters far more than either Gore or Kerry; he spoke on a simplistic, emotional level that resonated with voters; Gore and Kerry just didn't get it. And Gore's failure to align himself with the greatest economic boom in history was a gigantic mistake, as was Kerry's failure to explain his record in the Senate. And both Gore and Kerry came across as unfriendly, stiff, aloof, and uncomfortable, while Bush was more affable and relaxed. So demeanor in politics is perhaps more important than it is in business.

"Please don't misunderstand: I think that Bush is a brilliant communicator of selected messages. Gore and Kerry aren't."

"So articulation can win or lose elections, just as it can win or lose promotions on the job."

"Yes, the similarities and parallels are clear. Perhaps the practical applications, the details of everyday use, are less apparent.

"For example, as president of Berner International I addressed a homogeneous group; I think it's safe to assume that all employees are interested in the success of the company and continuation of their jobs. And most of them paid attention to what I was saying simply because I have some influence over their lives. I could be direct, not impolite or hurtful, but direct and to the point. I could explain fully any issue that we were discussing.

"Now, as a candidate, the issues are more diffuse and their implications far broader, and I often need to look for underlying messages when I'm asked a question. For example, the other day a constituent asked what I would do about all the terrorists living here in the U.S. I answered that I didn't think that many terrorists live here—not a good answer because this particular person was convinced there were. I failed to realize that the essence of her question was, 'what will you do to guarantee my safety?' That's a far broader issue, and my answer should have taken that into account with more far-reaching policy statements. So now when I'm asked a question I look for the hidden agenda, a way of asking myself if the question is the right one.

"On that same subject, I attended a meeting of the Democratic Women's Caucus not long ago, and someone asked the question: 'The Republicans are campaigning that they are now the party of faith and family and that Democrats have relinquished any claim to that position. What can we do about it?' My answer was that we never left our position and that we need to make our *continuing* support of faith and family a major campaign issue.

"I've also tweaked my personal definition of concise. As president of Berner, I could say or write as much as I needed to get my point across fully and clearly, including any rationale. And, if for some reason I wasn't clear, I was handed a second chance via employees' questions. Now, I'm part of the sound-bite society . . . any message over 30 words will probably be ignored, and 30 may be a high estimate. Voters expect candidates to cut to the quick, which of course forces us to distill our positions on even the most complex issues down to generalities that are quickly absorbed and can just as quickly be understood or misunderstood.

"And there's no way to change positions once they're out there, just as there's no way I can change my answer to the constituent who asked about terrorists. Sound bites are a fact of political life that can either help or hurt down the road; they can win or lose elections, as we know. I'll never forget Reagan's 'There you go again,' and I don't think many Americans of my generation will.

"So, to summarize the differences, demeanor, finding underlying meanings, choice of words, and concision may be a bit more important in politics than they are in business. Any similarities?"

"Absolutely. CLOWT applies everywhere, all the time. Clinton put compartmentalization into our language for a reason; it works. And, as we discussed earlier, you can't be an Articulate, regardless of your profession, without knowing how to listen, organize, write, and analyze feedback."

"Tell me, Georgia, you have had a wonderful career and life as a corporate executive. Why are you running for public office?"

"At the risk of sounding idealistic, I want to do what I can to reverse the many disturbing trends in government I see and deplore. A few specifics: the deficit is irresponsible, services needed for a civil society are being cut, and there's a general feeling that we as a nation are rudderless, without the overlying policies needed to establish directions that we can embrace.

"I sound-bite this down to our need to restore a sense of community . . . that feeling that we are all in this together, and by working together toward understandable, achievable goals, we can create a better society. We, of course, must articulate those goals and the means to reach them. I know I can help."

PART III

LET'S TALK MONEY, BIG MONEY!

If managers only knew: the costs of inarticulation and profits of articulation boggle the mind.

10 The High Costs of Inarticulation

If needless costs of 1 to 10 percent of sales impress you, read on.

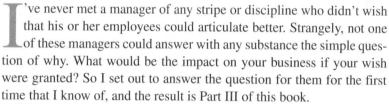

I've never met a manager of any stripe or discipline who didn't wish that his or her employees could articulate better. Strangely, not one of these managers could answer with any substance the simple question of why. What would be the impact on your business if your wish were granted? So I set out to answer the question for them for the first time that I know of, and the result is Part III of this book.

The fundamental conclusion is that inarticulation can cost a business 1 to 10 percent of sales. One corollary conclusion is that these costs, if eliminated, drop immediately and wholly to profits, and that profits can increase stock prices and improve bond ratings. A second corollary is that these costs can be converted to profits if managers and others change a few attitudes and behaviors.

Each reader must decide if my argument, which is based on anecdotal evidence, is compelling. I think most will if they relate their own experiences with the experiences of those who responded to my survey.

Each reader who finds my argument compelling must decide if a fix is in order. The reasons to do nothing are powerful psychological forces that lie within each of us; they must be recognized and exorcised before setting off on a course of action that transforms "bad" to "good" and costs to profits.

• • • •

An article published by *The Harvard Business Review* starts with these disheartening words: "What do businessmen answer when they are asked, 'What's the most troublesome problem you have to live with?' Frequently they reply, 'People just can't write. What do they learn in college now?'"[1]

The former president of a major manufacturer peered at me across his desk and confirmed, in a roundabout way, that college graduates, even those with higher degrees, haven't learned to communicate, especially to write. He told me that "the most frequent and vehement negative criticism from customers, and others, too, about employees at all levels is that they can't communicate! They can't talk in cohesive, coherent sentences. More important, they can't write, can't express their ideas on paper. We may have hired and trained a brilliant technical or analytical mind, but how would anyone know?"

"So what?" I asked, playing the role of devil's advocate. "How does your employees' inability to communicate, mainly to write, impact the revenues and profits of a business, which are the only things that managers seem to care about these days?"

"I don't know," he said, "but it must be big bucks."

So I set out to find out how many bucks equals "big." I first searched the libraries and the Internet for any prior research and came up empty. Then I surveyed the people I know who might have a handle on the answer.

I asked a dozen managers of communications and other functions this question: "How much, in your opinion, does inarticulation cost your company, or at least the part of the company that you manage?" Then I defined inarticulation as any communication that needs to be clarified by the receiver, igniting the telephone and other tag games with which we are so familiar, and which all of us have perpetrated many times in our careers. I defined inarticulation further as any communication that initiates actions that weren't intended by the sender, and any communication that alienates or loses a customer, requiring extraordinary sales efforts to either bring a customer back into the fold or develop a new one to fill in the gap. (I've said often that it costs 10 times more to develop a new customer than it does to keep an existing one. I'm now convinced that 10 times is far too low, and 50 to 100 times is more realistic, as several of the following anecdotes will confirm.)

Then I defined inarticulation even further: any communication by any employee that must be routinely edited or rewritten by a higher authority. In other words, any communication that can't be trusted to be clear, concise, and sensitive to the needs and feelings of readers and that doesn't fulfill the purposes of writers or readers.

AMAZINGLY CONSISTENT SURVEY RESPONSES

All the managers I approached considered the question carefully for a few minutes or days before responding. Most thought about the tag games and other unproductive efforts they had witnessed, then went to their calculators to figure the numbers and costs of wasted hours and dollars.

The bottom line of their responses: poor communication costs their businesses 1 to 10 percent of sales, *at least*. One said, "Certainly poor articulation as you define it costs us more than our gross profits. If we could eliminate it completely, we could double our earnings!" Another stared into his coffee as he swirled it in his cup, and said, "Poor articulation has cost us contracts, which we can get over, painful as it might be. It's also cost us customers, raising the pain level much higher. I fear sometimes that poor articulation could cost us our business! So the answer to your question is: surely more dollars than I'm willing to admit to."

The director of internal communications at a Fortune 500 company said flatly that poor communications cost his company at least 10 percent of sales, and that 10 percent seems optimistic. He then said that he could relate countless examples of communications from top executives that misdirected entire divisions, with staggering drops in productivity and profitability. And the director of a nationwide consulting firm said that poor writing has lost contracts and lost opportunities to negotiate premium prices on contracts already in house. He focused on loss of revenue and profits, not cost.

DO THESE ANECDOTES SOUND FAMILIAR?

Then I asked my interviewees to support their conclusions with a few examples, and I heard some horror stories that put the numbers in some perspective.

"Our engineering manager," said one, "wrote to all of our customers—we have only 18 of them, so losing one is a major setback—to explain a small defect in our product and how to repair it. Unfortunately, he worded his letter in a way that pinned the blame for the defect and the cost of fixing it on the customer. Very insensitive and certainly not our intent. Our customers, justifiably furious, called our president, who, also justifiably furious, set in motion a fix that surely cost the company tens of thousands of dollars more than it should have: he sent our engineering and sales managers to visit each customer and personally apologize for the letter, and then to supervise the repair of our product."

Another respondent told this story on himself: "I was head of our operations in Saudi Arabia and I wrote to the vice president back in the home office in the States, 'Do you want us to bid on the ABC job?' He cabled back, 'Yes, give it your best shot.' So I did, and spent literally hundreds of thousands of dollars on the bid. Unfortunately, my VP was thinking of another, much smaller project, and when he found out what I was bidding, he blew up. I explained to him that we were both victims of a communications snafu, which didn't help my reputation and pro-motability at all. Anyway, you can bet that I now make certain that my writing is far more specific and detailed. By the way, we didn't make the sale for the larger project, rubbing salt in the wound and severely hurting my career."

A division manager in a large engineering firm said to me, "We can't grow unless my project managers and engineers learn to write better. What they put on paper is so wordy, so poorly organized, so easily misunderstood that I live in fear that those awful words will somehow get into the hands of our customers. So I'm forced to edit every report, every proposal, every letter that goes out of here . . . and I admit to not being the greatest writer, editor, or diplomat the world has seen. The time I spend editing and cajoling is enormous, as is the time our engineers spend rewriting. That's time we should be doing what we know best: engineering. The loss in productivity is staggering!"

INARTICULATION ACCRUES MANY KINDS OF COSTS: A CONCERNED EXECUTIVE SPEAKS OUT

A vice president of a large engineering/construction company confided, "I see two prerequisites for being an Articulate, in particular for being a better writer, which I see as key. The first is clear thinking about the subject and the audience, which is absolutely necessary for the message to be logical, to flow easily from one topic to another, and to be sensitive to the needs of our clients. The second is the right attitude, which includes a willingness to at least consider suggestions for improvement without becoming defensive, and then to edit the text when the suggestions are constructive. This attitude is important whether the suggestions come from managers, peers, or customers.

"Inarticulation costs us dearly in several ways. First, there are the direct costs, the tag games that inevitably arise from murky or incomplete messages, and the revising needed to convert those messages to clear and complete before they're sent to a customer or to others in our company. Revising isn't disastrously expensive if the problems are syntactical or grammatical, which we can correct easily and quickly.

"Problems with structure, content, and tone are another matter; they're related directly to how our people think. Illogical, muddy thinking will always lead to illogical, muddy messages, and a patronizing attitude can set a tone that can destroy relationships that took us years or decades to build. These problems generally require that we start over from scratch, with a meeting of at least three of us to discuss what we're trying to say and to figure out why we didn't say it. Then someone is assigned to redo the report or whatever, which requires at least one more review meeting.

"Those costs can add up to 1 to 2 percent of sales, a very significant sum in this business where the highest profits we can expect range from 4 to 5 percent. So, if we could eliminate bad messages, we could raise profits by 20 to 50 percent.

"The costs don't stop there. Inarticulation can convert a good, competent, and profitable engineering job to a loser on all fronts: the client feels we did an inadequate job because he can't understand our message, and we've spent so much time revising that we've spent more than our profit.

"A second cost incurred is loss of business, in our case millions of dollars each year in revenue, and the loss of customers who take us off their bidders' lists because they cannot decipher our proposals or reports. One result is that our sales costs increase by hundreds of thousands of dollars each year—costs that directly erode our profits in a very significant way.

"Before I give you some examples, let me say that I am probably more aware of the need for clear, concise, and purposeful communications than most managers, and because of that awareness, I'd guess that our costs of inarticulation are lower than those same costs at comparable companies.

Every applicant for a job here that requires written or verbal contact with customers—and that includes all of our project engineers and construction superintendents—must submit with their résumé a sample of writing that they are particularly proud of. That sample is my first filter: poor grammar is grounds for suspicion that the applicant isn't right for us, and garbled writing, the kind that demonstrates poor thinking and is so expensive to fix, is grounds for rejection, despite their qualifications in other areas. We can't afford to hire people who can't articulate, and frankly, they can't afford to come with us. Poor writers in this company tend to be stuck in lower-level jobs that require little or no contact with customers, so if they're at all ambitious, they don't stick around very long.

"Despite our caution, Also-Rans somehow get on our payroll and they often hurt us before we either part company or we assign them to jobs that don't require communications. Here's an example of a covert Also-Ran. We negotiated a multimillion dollar contract to reduce the noxious air emissions from a foundry. The work was to proceed in three phases: (1) study conditions at the site and recommend remediation—a small, in terms of dollars, but critical step; (2) design and build the remediation plant, which would account for many millions of dollars, about 90 percent of our revenues; and (3) monitor the performance of the plant for two years to assure compliance with regulations.

"Armed with this contract, we very confidently promoted one of our best, most analytical design engineers to project engineer and sent him to the site, where he evaluated the situation. Returning to our offices, he wrote a report that, to be polite, was incomprehensible, baffling his immediate boss and then me. So the three of us met to figure out what to say to the customer—one of these meetings that ate up more than $500 an hour and should never have taken place.

"The engineer rewrote the report, and this time it was at least understandable, requiring only some simple edits. We overnighted it to the customer, who called our engineer a day later. Their conversation went something like this:

Customer:	This report has nothing to do with our plant. It's all wrong. Are you sure it isn't meant for another customer?
Engineer:	Can't be. That report reflects what I saw at your plant. You aren't reading it carefully. Try it again.
Customer:	I've read it three times. I still don't see how this report applies to us.
Engineer:	Well it does. I was there. I should know.

"The customer hung up, called me, and told me that our firm obviously did not understand his company's problems or needs, and that we sent an engineer to review the situation who not only does not understand the technical aspect of the problem, but is so defensive about his writing that he insults the intelligence of customers. He then cancelled our contract—costing us millions in lost revenues—and refused to pay for costs incurred so far, more than $100,000. Then, to top it off, he refused to send us any requests for proposals for 18 months. We not only lost the opportunity to bid on several millions of dollars' worth of new work, but we spent many thousands in sales costs to win him back.

"The day after our contract was cancelled—I wanted a day to cool off—I met with our engineer one more time and pointed out the inaccuracies in his report as explained to me by the customer. Strangely, he agreed that the report wasn't accurate. When I asked why he allowed it to be sent to the customer anyway, he replied that he didn't want to spend any more of the company's money on rewriting and that he found it boringly difficult to cover the same ground over and over. That engineer is no longer with us, which I'm sure isn't surprising.

"Sometimes the client's poor writing can cost as much or more than our own. Not long ago, we were invited, along with four other firms, to bid on the design and construction of a large power plant. Many details in the request for proposal—the RFP—were ambiguous, requiring interpretation, which, in our business, is a two-bit word meaning 'guesswork.' Not surprisingly, there were huge differences in the scopes of work and prices among the five proposals, so the customer called a meeting at the site, a remote area in the western U.S. The ambiguities were hashed out over three days, and the client, who finally saw the problem, elected to cancel all bids and rewrite the RFP, which was reissued about a year later. I can only guess at the client's cost, but it had to be hundreds of thousands of dollars to redo the RFP, and much more in additional site visits and lost revenue. My estimate of the cost to the bidders approaches $2 million dollars; our direct costs alone were well over $400,000."

CONFESSIONS OF A PROFESSIONAL WRITER

I've been active in the communications business for more than 30 years—a professional writer for all sorts of companies—and I communicate most often and regularly with people working for large and small businesses who carry titles like communications manager. We should be able to communicate clearly and concisely with each other and avoid the mishaps cited earlier, but we can't, don't, or won't. In fact, I am constantly amazed at how often we fall into the same traps as the people who hire us and how much it costs us and our clients. Here's just one example.

I read an op-ed piece in the local newspaper in which a Rand Corporation study was cited. I checked the Internet under Rand without finding any reference to this particular study, so:

- I called the author (the president of a nearby college) and told his secretary what I wanted. She told me that the president would call me ([1] on Figure 1).
- The president shuffled my request to the college's public information (PI) officer. [2] A week later . . .
- The PI officer called [3] and, in a garbled message on my answering machine, told me that a fax [4] is on the way. (He later explained that he was talking to somebody in his office while talking to my answering machine, which distracted him and, he figured, excused his garblings. I'm not joking. And to reiterate a point made earlier, this is further proof that multitasking is a hoax.)
- The fax referred me to a magazine in which a synopsis of the study supposedly appeared. I couldn't find the magazine on the Internet or at the local library [5].
- Thinking that I had missed something, I called the administrative assistant [6] at the university where I teach and asked her to locate, either on the Web or at the library [7], the magazine and study. She e-mailed me: [8] "Sorry, there's no such magazine."
- I phoned the administrative assistant [9] to determine the problem, without resolution. So—
- I called the PI officer [10], who chuckled and said, "You should know that you can't trust anyone who writes his own faxes." In that one sentence he raised defensiveness to a new level by immediately and callously blaming me for his shortcomings as a communicator, placing him solidly among the Also-Rans described in this book. Then he told me that he had cited a nonexistent journal, gave me the correct name, and offered to contact his public rela-

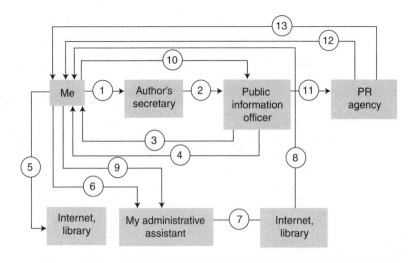

Figure 1. A simple request for supporting data for a short op-ed piece set off a 13-step tangled web of connections that wasted 3 1/2 to 4 hours and most likely cost more than $600. How many times are similar or more complex tangled webs created in the typical company? In your company?

tions (PR) agency in another city and have someone fax me a copy of the article. Weary of playing tag, I agreed.

- He called his agency [11], after which an agency person called [12] to say the fax was on its way. The fax arrived [13]—more than two weeks after my request.

Lost time:

Me:	At least an hour
The president's secretary:	1/2 hour
PI officer:	1/2 hour
The administrative assistant:	1/2 hour
The librarian:	1/2 hour
The PR agency:	1/2 hour
Total unproductive time and added cost:	3 1/2 to 4 hours and at least $600

Note

1. John Fielden, "What Do You Mean I Can't Write?" in *The Articulate Executive* (Boston: HBS Press, 1991).

11 The High Profits of Articulation

The high costs of inarticulation convert neatly to profits.

If inarticulation costs 1 to 10 percent of sales, it follows that converting all of it to articulation can raise profits by that same amount and that stock prices will follow suit. Here are some anecdotes to support that contention.

"My articulation was key to winning the biggest order in the history of the business . . . millions of dollars for six of the largest turbine generators ever built," said the marketing manager of a large manufacturer. "Our customer was a consortium of international electric utilities, and the purchasing decision would be made by a committee chaired by the head of a hostile firm who seemed always to be living up to his reputation as the toughest, hardest-nosed negotiator.

"Anyway, our most formidable competitor wrote a letter to the committee that described, point by point, the alleged problems with our machines. It was lousy writing because it was based on information that was just plain outdated or wrong. For example, the last 'problem' couldn't possibly be related to our machines, so it was clear to me that the writers were confused. Regardless, they broke a cardinal rule for articulation: know the subject before creating the message.

"I wrote a five-page letter that rebutted their points one at a time and in the same order to make the two letters easy to compare. I worked on that letter for a couple of days, collecting supporting data, making sure I was being clear and that my tone wasn't at all defensive or disparaging—

except when I got to the last point, where I noted quite strongly that I couldn't comment on another manufacturer's machine.

"A month or so later my project team and I were in a meeting with the committee. The chairman raised his arms and waved my letter at me and asked if I had written it. I admitted that, yes, I had, knowing that I had done a good job. After asking a few questions, the chairman thanked us for being so thorough with both our written and spoken responses and terminated the meeting. A week later we booked the order."

• • • •

"Forceful writing pulled our business out of its self-defeating rut," reported a division manager of a large consulting firm. "We were headed for disaster, even extinction, if we couldn't change our attitudes toward customers and our own professionalism. So I wrote a memo with the sole purpose of shaking up the troops and setting us on a better path. Here's one part of the memo: 'Reports with poor clarity, coherence, and continuity; proposals with poorly defined scopes of work or lack of any innovation; and the widespread tendency to cut and paste past boiler-plate documents to meet the *individual needs* of our clients are examples of a few of the major items that reflect our *attitude* toward our clients. Typographical errors, lack of response to phone calls, failure to follow up on simple requests are a few examples of the lack of attention to details that lead to dissatisfied clients.'

"I said in my memo that, against my wishes and contrary to my normal and softer management style of persuasion and cooperation, I would be 'Gestapo-like' in my demands. I reluctantly went so far as to threaten each employee by saying, 'We will have serious reservations of retaining anyone who doesn't change his or her attitude.' I guess you could say that my tone was demanding in that it reflected my own frustration with what had become a desperate situation. I certainly was not diplomatic, and I didn't pull any punches.

"Anyway, it worked. Most of my people shaped up; a few didn't and were replaced. The business grew and became profitable as customers' dissatisfaction turned to satisfaction during the following year, evidence of the power of articulation.

"Here's more evidence for any skeptics: I know that my memo still lurks in the desk drawers of many current and former employees. I've seen them peek at it to remind themselves to never fall into those awful habits of what we now refer to as the 'bad old days.' "

• • • •

"Articulation cuts both ways," related a top manager of an environmental engineering company. "Our most important products are proposals and reports, and both must reflect our intelligence, our insights into our customers' problems, and the solutions we recommend. When they don't— well, we can kiss that job or customer goodbye. So part of our hiring process is a writing test, which sometimes doesn't work as we'd like.

"We hired an engineer with a very fine academic background and, we thought, pretty good writing skills. We were half right. His first report was garbled, a bunch of nonsense that, frankly, would have embarrassed us terribly if the customer got hold of it.

"I read it on a Saturday and it was just good fortune that my new employee wasn't there, I was so dismayed and angry. I calmed down, commented on the piece, edited it a bit, called a meeting on Monday to talk it over, and sent our guy back to his word processor.

"Meanwhile, I called our customer, who was already pressing us pretty hard, and told him that his report would be late because we were checking on some data—a little white lie, of course. A few days later the engineer came back with what he thought was a new draft. In fact, he had made the small editing changes I suggested but neglected all my comments about structure, coherence, and just plain sense.

"Then it dawned on me. This engineer wasn't 'seeing' writing as a series of connected thoughts. Nonsense somehow made sense to him. I rewrote the report myself, seething with every word I wrote, with every minute I wasted, and with my own inability to recognize his inability to write before I hired him.

"This is a bad-news, good-news story. On the bad side, we let the engineer go, had to, simply because we cannot tolerate the drop in productivity and higher costs that he caused. On the good side, he is now a lab scientist with another company and I'm sure is doing fine. And I'm even more careful to hire people who can write.

"There's more. Our client liked the final report so much that he called to say that he wanted to discuss it in my office. Turned out he was using the report as a reason to tour our facilities and meet some of our principals. The result was a large, long-term contract that we were awarded because he was confident that we could do a good job and further his career at the same time.

"Does articulation affect careers? You bet, of both senders and receivers."

• • • •

"The first rule of articulation is to play to the audience," reported a sales engineer for a manufacturer of heavy equipment for the mining industry. "I met with a potential client for several hours before writing a proposal and during the meeting was able to uncover the hot buttons that would sell the job. My proposal hit them all, prompting one member of the evaluation team to ask if I had an insider 'mole' on my payroll.

"'Your price is high,' said my customer, 'but don't fret. Your proposal offers exactly what we want, while the others miss the mark. Here's your purchase order.'"

• • • •

"Good writing helped me get almost $100,000 in scholarships and grants," said a graduate student at a major university, "and I couldn't have finished my education without them.

"I first became aware of the direct connection between good writing and success while in high school, when it became very clear that good writing led to better grades. Then, when I applied to colleges, I connected good writing to financial gain when I was awarded a full scholarship based on my grades and my clear statement of goals and interests. The connection continued in graduate school, where again I was awarded a full scholarship plus a major stipend for continuing research, both based on my clearly written description of my goals.

"My college career is a testament to the benefits of good writing. My message to all parents is simply this: teach your kids to be articulate, especially to write well, and reap the rewards."

• • • •

I uncovered any number of other stories about the many benefits of articulation. For example, I talked to a marketing manager who differentiated his products from competitors' with a clear statement of features and their benefits; another who defined the value inherent in his products in a new way, creating a new purchasing decision tree that increased his company's market share and profits; and an executive who insists on perfect proposals and reports because he knows that they are key to opening new accounts and to repeat business, and so on.

The bottom lines? There are several. On a personal level, there's no question that there's a direct connection between articulation and promotability. You may be the most brilliant engineer, manager, scientist, accountant, or whatever, but nobody will know that if your skills are hiding behind murky prose. Witness the new hire and the student in the anecdotes presented earlier.

There's also no question that articulation is good for business—any business that must communicate with customers, employees, stockholders, and so on. Only articulation can differentiate the business, its products, and its expertise from those of competitors.

12

A Glance at the Root Causes of Inarticulation and How They Can Be Reversed

The causes and cures lie within each of us.

The anecdotes in Chapter 11 aren't unique or even unusual. Businesspersons who honestly examine their business processes can relate all sorts of horror stories about poor communications and how they erode productivity, revenues, profits, stock prices, and relations with customers and employees.

Yet, despite the validity of these anecdotes, it's astounding to me that I have met only a handful of businesspersons who are willing to face the huge costs of inarticulation and at least attempt to correct the causes. Why? I see four reasons (I'm sure you can point to others), all based on the insights of experience (see Figure 2).

First, communications are "soft," with costs that are difficult to measure precisely, yet everyone knows they are endemic. On the other hand, productivity in an office or plant and quality of a product or service are "hard"—that is, easier to measure. So, goes the reasoning, improve productivity and quality where it can be measured more easily, and tell the world about it with chest-pounding rhetoric. It's easier, and maybe it's good for the ego, but is it more beneficial to the bottom line? Is it a hangover from that awful and wrong aphorism of a few decades ago: if you can't measure it, you can't manage it? Try to measure the contributions of accountants and lawyers to the bottom line.

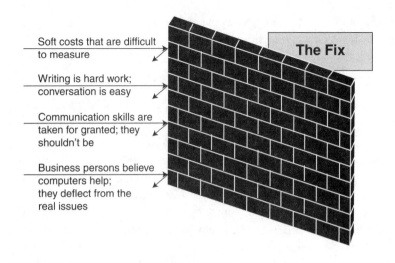

Soft costs that are difficult to measure

Writing is hard work; conversation is easy

Communication skills are taken for granted; they shouldn't be

Business persons believe computers help; they deflect from the real issues

The Fix

Figure 2. Managers cite many excuses for not taking the necessary steps to improve the writing of employees—four of them are shown here.

Second, being articulate is hard work—very hard—as Jim Browne points out in Chapter 5. The disciplines of writing, for example, force thinking to depths that we can avoid in conversation. Yet, it's exactly those disciplines that are most valuable to businesspeople who search for greater clarity, who want deeper insights into complex concepts such as strategies and marketing positions, and who want to discover the important connections among facts, ideas, and systems that otherwise may remain undiscovered.

Third, managers avoid the issue of inarticulation because, for some reason, skills in communications in general and writing in particular are taken for granted. After all, we have all been communicating all our lives and we've made it this far. (Perhaps it's time for all of us to quit congratulating ourselves for our successes and consider how far we might have gotten if only we were more articulate.) Yet, as I pointed out earlier, managers complain loud and long about the writing of their employees, creating a paradox with, apparently, the lifeline of Methuselah.

There's another related and perhaps more personal reason for avoidance: managers, highly competent in their fields, feel totally unable to critique an employee's writing beyond very general comments like "it isn't clear" or "it doesn't sound right." Their instincts are probably on target, but they cannot support them with the specifics needed to be helpful to the writer. So, rather than embarrass themselves with abstractions, they don't say anything.

Last, many businesspersons honestly cling to the belief that computers help their people communicate. That's an illusion—a dangerous illusion at that, because it deflects us from the real issues of clear thinking, precise wording, and empathy for readers. Nevertheless, spell-check, grammar check, and other similar tools are valuable assets for writers if they are used in conjunction with clear thinking and critical reading. Russell E. Eshleman Jr. agrees: "[Students not attending classes] would miss my tirades about the evils of spell check and grammar check on their computers. Those dastardly devices have become crutches that they rely on too much . . . and let them down too much. What's a buoy to dew?"[1]

The bottom line is that computers can speed up communications, but they can't eliminate poor communications as I've defined them. Only that age-old computer, the human mind, can do that.

But admonishing the human mind to articulate better is counterproductive at best. Such admonishment would likely hurt, disappoint, and alarm most people who hear those words, because they are basically so meaningless and damaging to morale that their writing becomes more ineffectual than ever.

More meaningful and far more constructive would be specific suggestions concerning how and why to articulate better.

MOVING FROM BAD TO BETTER TO GOOD

If you've read this far, you've likely moved beyond idle curiosity to recognizing that your experiences with bad writing parallel to some extent the experiences of those persons who contributed to this part of the book. And you're wondering what can be done to avoid those experiences in the future.

I see three paths on which it's possible to move from bad to better to good: hire people who are competent in their main field as well as in articulation (pretty rare birds), train employees, or retain a consultant (see Figure 3). Consider these principles before starting down one of these paths:

1. Realize and understand that almost anybody can become more articulate by implementing CLOWT and the Elite Eleven Tools (see Chapter 14); you and those around you aren't condemned to inarticulation.

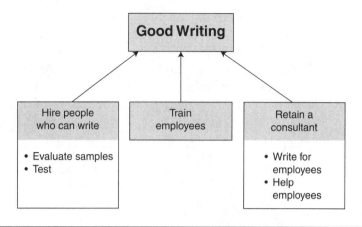

Figure 3. Only three paths to good writing are available to managers; regardless of the path or paths selected, managers should consider the five principles mentioned in the text.

2. Understand that, above all else, articulation is a reflection of thinking (not of an innate ability to string pretty-sounding sentences together), so it follows that you should select and train your clearest, most logical thinkers to be your most visible communicators. In that way, you stand a better chance of avoiding the tag games and other productivity busters that are so costly.

3. Focus on training in the five fundamental behaviors of articulation (CLOWT), the Elite Eleven Tools, and other tools you'll find in any good book on writing, a few of which are noted in the bibliography. Then insist that all employees—top managers especially—practice all the habits and use the tools until they become so internalized that they are second nature.

4. Avoid training that focuses on the mechanics of writing, the nitpicks of punctuation and grammar; it's almost always a waste of time and money. Yes, mechanics are important, but studying them can actually worsen articulation by deflecting employees from the essential elements of thinking and meaning. Instead, for those employees who communicate with others, buy each employee a handbook for writers (mostly grammar) and a handbook of English usage (mostly the meanings and uses of troublesome words). The librarian at a local university can recommend several titles, or you can refer to the bibliography. Then insist

that employees who write refer to the books whenever they are unsure about where to put a comma, when to replace a comma with a semicolon, the proper usage of a word, and so on.

5. And last, commit for the long term: Articulates can be made, but not overnight, any more than good engineers, accountants, computer specialists, or any other professional can be made overnight. In fact, it could take longer to make a good writer simply because so many bad habits may need to be exorcised.

Note

1. Russell E. Eshleman Jr., *Pittsburgh Post Gazette*, December 12, 2004.

PART IV
SELF-HELP FOR BELIEVERS

*If you've read this far and aren't
a believer, one of us has failed.*

13 Painless (Almost) Ways to Build Your Vocabulary

It's almost too easy to create such a powerful competitive advantage.

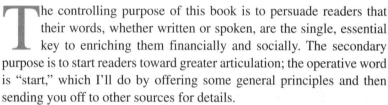

The controlling purpose of this book is to persuade readers that their words, whether written or spoken, are the single, essential key to enriching them financially and socially. The secondary purpose is to start readers toward greater articulation; the operative word is "start," which I'll do by offering some general principles and then sending you off to other sources for details.

To that end, be assured that my suggestions for building your vocabulary and the Elite Eleven Tools for writing clearly and concisely have proven their mettle on the many and varied battlegrounds of business and other parts of life—the real world in which you live.

Many universities and consultants offer proven methods for building vocabularies that are customized for various ages and levels in the organization. For example, one consultant offers self-help procedures for entry-level employees, middle managers, and top executives. Still others offer methods by grade levels. Interested readers will find dozens of choices by searching "vocabulary building" on the Internet.

The executives profiled in this book have developed habits that, as one told me, "keep [his] verbal skills sharp." He and others use word-a-day calendars on which to keep their schedules, and they actually use the daily word in writing or talking to embed it into their lexicon. Many also complete at least one crossword a day because, as one said to me, "It forces me to learn the more obscure meanings of words and to cross-reference meanings in my mind." One told me that he feels that something is missing from his life if he doesn't work the two crosswords and the Jumble in the daily paper. He also confesses to usually being "in the middle of" at least one larger and more complex puzzle.

Still another is addicted to Scrabble; she "always has a game or two going" with her husband or kids. They stop and start as their schedules dictate, which "massages our memories as well as our vocabularies."

All are insatiable readers of what they call "the good stuff": reputable trade journals and business magazines, business books, the occasional novel, and well-regarded newspapers such as the *New York Times* and the *Wall Street Journal*, which actually dig deep enough into a subject to be useful. They leaf through local newspapers to catch the flavor of what's going on in their immediate surroundings, and they never waste time on letters to editors or highly biased editorials. As they read, they note unfamiliar words or familiar words used in a newer context and then look them up in a handy dictionary and add them to their stash.

All know that the need to expand their vocabularies never ends if they are to continue advancing their professional and personal lives. They also are positive role models for the many people around them and are fully aware that exercising their minds is the best way to fend off Alzheimer's and other mental handicaps as they age.

14 The Elite Eleven Tools for Becoming an Articulate

Habituate CLOWT and these 11 tools and you're on the road to becoming an Articulate.

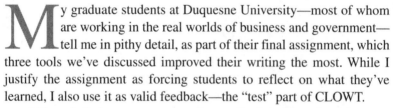

My graduate students at Duquesne University—most of whom are working in the real worlds of business and government—tell me in pithy detail, as part of their final assignment, which three tools we've discussed improved their writing the most. While I justify the assignment as forcing students to reflect on what they've learned, I also use it as valid feedback—the "test" part of CLOWT.

Although their answers vary all over the lot, they also take on a pattern and can be "chunked." (See "2. Super-Glue Your Topics.") One student said she discovered the semicolon (see "7. Dash to the Dashing Dash"), and another found new respect for readers' sensibilities ("1. You Can't Communicate if You Can't Empathize" and others). Several said they improved so much that they had been "anointed" official editors for their businesses and couldn't decide to thank or curse me.

I've gathered their answers into this chapter, presenting you the tools that my students and others say solved 80 percent of their articulation problems. That's practical knowledge you can use today, tomorrow, and forever, as long as you can peck a keyboard or utter a word. (It's also knowledge that every writer or teacher of writing can dispute. All, I assume, have their pet lists of what works and what doesn't. This list is mine.)

Here's the drill.

1. YOU CAN'T COMMUNICATE IF YOU CAN'T EMPATHIZE

Yup, the first step toward articulation is exactly what your fifth-grade teacher told you: know your audience, get into your audience's minds, and fantasize how they will react to your words. Unfortunately, your teacher probably didn't tell you how to get that knowledge, a deficiency we'll correct right now.

Here are several ways to dig deeper into the minds of your readers and listeners to connect with them more tightly by shaping, just for them, the content (what you choose to say), structure (the order in which to say it), and tone (the words you use) of your important message. (By the way, content, structure, and tone are three essential characteristics of all writing.)

First, complete the following reader profile before starting to write, no matter how trivial the task or message may be. Do that for at least the next two months, after which the profile will be embedded in your psyche and will be second nature to you.

Then, after completing the profile, lean back and think about your answers and how they affect content, structure, and tone. For example, suppose you're writing about a new electronic circuit breaker for homes, a new device that greatly raises protection against electrical fires. If your readers are electrical engineers who specify such devices, you might explain the technology in some detail (content), explain it early in the piece (structure), and use all the technical jargon at your command (tone). If your readers are homeowners, you'd likely explain the benefits first (content and structure), using layman's language (tone); technology would be touched on, if mentioned at all.

The profile is as follows:

1. Primary reader(s): Names/titles
2. Secondary reader(s): Names/titles
3. The purpose(s) of the document: the changes in thinking or behavior that you want (to affect content, structure, and tone)
4. Key points (to affect content and structure):
   - Main
   - Supporting

5. Readers know the subject (to affect content, structure, and tone):
   - Well
   - A little
   - Not at all
6. Readers know the technology (to affect tone):
   - Well
   - A little
   - Not at all
7. Based on readers' knowledge of the subject and technology, the tone should be:
   - Detailed
   - General
   - Technical
   - Lay
8. Readers' feelings toward the subject (to affect tone):
   - Hostile
   - Resentful
   - Wary
   - Accepting
9. Readers' feelings toward the writer (to affect tone):
   - Hostile
   - Resentful
   - Wary
   - Accepting

Related to the profile is the Ten Minute Drill, which I guarantee will improve your writing. For each assignment, take 10 minutes to:

1. Complete the audience profile in writing; one-word answers are sufficient.
2. Contemplate how and why your answers will impact content, structure, and tone.
3. Fix on the key points; select the one or two that are most important to you and the reader; start your piece with those points.
4. Order the other points by importance.

Then . . .

5. Sketch out a first draft without considering grammar or syntax; put your thoughts on paper in the order you've selected. Start

writing the details and work toward the abstract. In other words, reverse the order you've been taught and start with the body of the piece (or an appendix if there is one), not the executive summary. Write your table of contents last.

6. Put the piece aside for hours, days if possible, to let your subconscious smarts kick in. See "11. Start Early on Every Communications Assignment" for more on this vital point.

7. Rewrite often by referring to your profile. Nobody's first draft is right, and nobody's final draft is perfect, but rewriting can move it as close as possible.

8. Consider the piece complete when it is true to the profile.

2. SUPER-GLUE YOUR TOPICS

To prevent the confusion and irritation caused by jumping around and creating a stew of thoughts, keep your topics together—writers call it "chunk" and "unity." Lists—whether bulleted when there isn't a clear hierarchy of thoughts or sequence of events, or numbered when there is—can help to chunk.

This sentence is from a short proposal written by a marketing manager at a large consulting firm: "Our scope of work includes specifications for high alumina bricks, magnesia alumina spinel brick, steel fiber reinforced castables, acid resistant castables, and direct bonded magnesia chrome brick."

The topics move from brick and bricks—is plural or singular correct?—to castables, then back to brick, creating a disunity: a move from subject A to subject B and then back to subject A. I like to think of disunity as a sandwich: bread, baloney, bread. This sentence is also replete with tiresome redundancy: how many times must the reader read "brick" or "castables"? Isn't once enough?

Try a bulleted list:

Our scope of work includes specifications for the following:
- Bricks: high alumina, magnesia alumina spinel, and direct bonded chrome; and
- Castables: steel fiber reinforced and acid resistant.

Now the main topics, bricks and castables, are chunked, and the reader easily knows what the work will be.

Suppose for a moment that you, the writer, prefer prose instead of a list for whatever reason. The exercise of creating a list is still valuable to help chunk, and the list can be easily reversed to understandable prose: *Our scope of work includes specifications for bricks (high alumina, magnesia alumina spinel, and direct bonded chrome) and castables (steel fiber reinforced and acid resistant).*

A perfect disunity was unwittingly written by a candidate for a master's degree who was unlucky enough to draw a writer on his review committee:

> Along with economic changes, the large utility boilers that are utilized in the power generating process are highly regulated from an environmental perspective. The electrical power producing industry is the largest contributor of pollutant emissions to the air and water. Because of this, this industry is highly regulated at the state and federal levels.

The topics bounce from highly regulated to largest contributor to highly regulated again, creating that perfect sandwich that good writers avoid. A better way to express the same thoughts is the following:

> Electricity generators emit more air and water pollutants than any other industry. Therefore, they are regulated heavily by state and federal governments.

Chunking helped to drop the number of words by about half, from 45 to 22, creating concision and clarity in one smart move.

3. THINK DOMINOES

Be absolutely certain that one thought leads logically to the next. Articulates call this "cohesion" or "tracking"; readers call it "clear." Here's a memo from a VP that bounces all over the lot and is wordy beyond comprehension:

I would like to take this opportunity to formally announce that effective August 1, 2004, Jim Smith has accepted the position of Manager, Business Development. In this position, Jim will be responsible for leading the Utility Group's marketing and business development efforts for the utility contractor market segment.

As a former manager with both ABC and XYZ, Jim comes to this position with extensive experience supporting both the utility and contractor market segments, and he will be responsible for the continued development and implementation of the Utility Group's strategic business plan for the utility contractor marketing segment.

In this position Jim's duties will include, but are not limited to, providing the leadership and management direction necessary to successfully conduct the business development effort, major proposal development, key contract negotiations, strategic regional and national procurement and materials management program implementations, and the activities associated with implementing any regional and national programs focused on the utility contractor market segment.

Additionally, Jim will work closely with the Directors of Operations, the Utility Group's Sales Directors and Utility Account representatives in the development, implementation and tracking of their branch specific business and sales plans focused on the support and growth of utility contractor business at the branch level.

The first two sentences move from announcement to duties; the second paragraph moves from experience to duties in one sentence. The third and fourth paragraphs stick to duties in a long string—a signal that a list may be needed to tidy up the mess. In addition, the words are so convoluted and redundant that readers found it impossible to figure out what poor Jim will actually be doing.

These 308 words of verbose confusion can be boiled down to 100 words of concise clarity by using a bulleted list and not miss a single thought:

Jim Smith has been appointed manager, business development, Utility Group, effective August 1, 2004. A former senior manager at ABC and XYZ, Jim brings extensive experience to the marketing and business development efforts to expand our participation in the utility contractor market segment.

Jim will be responsible for development and implementation of the Group's strategic business plan. Specifically, he will:

- Negotiate key contracts;
- Implement strategic and national programs, including those related to national procurement and materials management; and
- Cooperate with utility account representatives at branches to develop, implement, and track sales plans that support growth.

Which version do you prefer? Which version do you think the thousands of busy and interested employees who were forced to wade through it would prefer?

4. PUT TOGETHER PARAGRAPHS WITH PIZZAZZ

Use the ABC structure that every reader looks for: Abstract (topic sentence that tees up your readers and tells them what to expect, often referred to as the controlling idea), Body (the meat of your story, which explains and expands on the controlling idea), and Conclusion (tell them what you want them to leave with).

The topic sentence must present both a subject and an attitude toward the subject. "Pete wrote a book" is far too broad for a good topic sentence, and where's the attitude? "Pete wrote a book that convinced me to build my vocabulary" is more explicit because it includes attitude. You can support the sentence with details from the book, and you can even draw conclusions.

Another simple example to seat the concept: "Pittsburgh is a pleasant city in which to live" is too broad and doesn't offer an attitude. It literally demands a long litany of supporting attributes that would fill a book, and has. So, let's add attitude: "Pittsburgh is a pleasant city in which to live largely because of its professional football team, the Steelers." Now the topic sentence can be supported by the successes and failures—or just the most recent to trim the subject even further—of the team and its influences on city life.

These two paragraphs were written by a respected consultant to entice chemists and others to attend his seminars:

The course leader is Dr. ABC, he has 34 years of MS experiences in many problem solving applications: environmental sciences, clinical, toxicology, forensics, legal and illegal drugs, natural products, metabolism, food sciences, R&D, biotechnology and others [1]. Required text is IOM fourth edition by XYZ. This book must be brought to your course and purchased from: University Books, 20 South Street, Anycity, PA, telephone DEF or fax GHI [2]. This course will cover most of the problems in the first five chapters and additional selected subjects [3]. Please note your experiences and special interests on the registration form below [4].

Register by making a copy of this form and sending it with a check for $$$ to secure your attendance. Hotel information and a map will be sent to confirm your registration. Please list your special interest on the registration form below [5]. Enrollment is limited, to assure maximum course benefits [6]. On-site courses are available [7], call YYY for further information. We also provide laboratory services [8].

A short outline of the main ideas in each sentence, plus a few comments, demonstrates how the subjects bounce around, creating disunity and confusion: [1] consultant's qualifications, the topic sentence that is dropped immediately as the writer moves posthaste to another subject; [2] textbook, with the impression that it must be purchased from one store; [3] course content; [4] applicant's interests; [5] register/cost and applicant's interests again, a redundancy sure to irritate the careful and busy reader; [6] register soon, smacking of pressure selling; [7] other courses that are unrelated to this one; and [8] other services, also unrelated to this one and an obvious attempt to broaden the sales pitch.

This jumble of thoughts indicates a jumbled mind or, at the very least, a lazy one—not the image any consultant would nourish or cherish.

Chunking and separating the main thoughts, and remembering the purpose, leads to this:

> Your course leader, Dr. ABC, offers 34 years practical experience in MS and related disciplines: environmental and food sciences, clinical toxicology, metabolism (including the effects of legal drugs and natural products), biotechnology, and others. He is an accomplished R&D scientist and entertaining speaker. "I really enjoyed the class and learned a lot at the same time," noted one recent attendee.
>
> Your text, IOM, fourth edition, by XYZ, can be purchased at most bookstores for $$$. To optimize your benefits, please bring the book with you to all classes.
>
> The course will cover all the topics addressed in the first five chapters of the text, plus other related topics, some of which will be determined by your preferences noted on your registration form.
>
> To register, complete a copy of the form below and mail it as soon as possible; attendance is limited to assure personal attention to everyone.
>
> Other, related courses offered by Dr. ABC are described on (website) and include laboratory analyses.

5. YANK YOUR WORDS OFF THEIR LAZY DUFFS

Use the active voice and exorcise those couch-potato words that afflict readers with a terminal case of the nods. But don't forget passive voice; it has its places. Writers prefer the active voice because it adds a sense of punch and motion to the document, and it typically requires one-third fewer words.

Some definitions: in *active voice*, the subject of a sentence performs the action; in *passive voice*, the subject is acted upon (has something done to it). "Pete wrote a book" is active because the subject, Pete, performs the act of writing. "The book was written by Pete" is passive because the subject, book, is acted upon by Pete. Note that the active sentence is only four words, one-third fewer than the six in the passive sentence, and the active is clearer.

A more complex example: "The board suggested that the project manager revise the schedule" is active and 10 words. "It was suggested by the board that the schedule be revised by the project manager" is passive and 15 words.

Preferring active voice doesn't mean that writers must use it all the time. Passive voice has its legitimate uses—for example, when the performer isn't known or relevant, or when the emphasis is on the receiver of the action. "The mayor was hit by a tomato during the rally" is properly passive because the mayor is presumably more important than the tomato and should be at the beginning of the sentence. The active version of the same thought would be: "A tomato hit the mayor," which cuts the number of words from 10 to 5 but relegates the poor mayor to second place.

A rule of thumb to check if you are using passive too often is that effective business writing is 65 percent or more active, 35 percent or less passive. Many word processing programs will calculate the percentages for you.

6. BREATHE NEW LIFE INTO DROWSY NOUNS THAT CAN BE SCRAPPY VERBS

Deadly, useless, vague, and pointless corporate babble fills pages but fails to positively influence the minds that influence your career. Avoid such wordy and murky sentences as "He issued his authorization for the project" when "He authorized the project" will do the job better. Note that I changed "authorization," a noun, to "authorize," a verb. Another example: "We insist on proper utilization of our support services" can be "Utilize our support services properly." "Her performance exceeded expectations" can be "She performed beyond expectations."

Some other nouns that can be verbs include the following: illustration (illustrate), implementation (implement), advancement (advance), realization (realize), transmittal (transmit), confrontation (confront), documentation (document), negotiation (negotiate), concession (concede), quotation (quote), employment (employ), determination (determine), relation (relate), and administration (administer).

7. DASH TO THE DASHING DASH

The dash and its kissin' cousins—the comma, semicolon, and colon—are your friends if you know how to play 'em, your enemies if you don't.

This can help: think of punctuation as driving your car. Use a comma when coming to a rolling stop, a semicolon for a slower stop, a colon for an almost complete stop, and a period for a full stop. Use a dash to replace a comma, semicolon, or colon whenever you want to set off a thought—make it stand out—and when the thought is clearly parenthetical, that is, not essential to the central message. Then follow these few rules; they cover 80 percent of the situations you'll likely encounter in business (note the semicolon and colon in this sentence):

A. Use a comma between all words in a series, including the last one—the one preceded by "and" or "or"—called the serial comma. Using the serial comma adds clarity by avoiding such sentences as "The inheritance will be divided equally between Tom, Ann, Sam and Joan," which could make Sam and Joan very unhappy. Exception: Don't place a comma between inseparable pairs such as ham and eggs, peanut butter and jelly, love and marriage, and Bonnie and Clyde.

B. Use a comma before conjunctions—"and," "but," and "with" are the most common—when connecting independent clauses (clauses with a subject and a predicate that express a complete thought). Use a semicolon if you don't want to use a conjunction, as I did in the lead-in sentence to this list. And use a semicolon to connect two independent clauses that express thoughts that are closely connected; that is, they need to be closer than they would be if they were separated by a period.

C. Use a comma to separate an introductory phrase from the rest of the sentence—For example, . . . In addition, . . . As I mentioned, . . . Furthermore, . . . However, . . . and others that are commonly used as transitions to smooth and alert readers to the logical flow of thoughts.

D. Use a colon to pay off the thought to its left in the sentence with the thought to the right; the payoff is often a list. For example, "Joe wants four gifts for his birthday: a tie, a sweater, a hat, and a football."

8. FINE-TUNE YOUR POOP DETECTOR

Become a more careful reader to spot the miscues in your and others' work; then become a ruthless editor to fix the goofs the way they should be fixed. Ernest Hemingway said that the first prerequisite for becoming a good writer is to develop a built-in, infallible poop (he used stronger language) detector. I'd add the following: for your own words as well as for others'.

Here's an example from a direct-mail flyer trying to entice me into buying a book: "In *The Sociopath Next Door*, psychologist Martha Stout dissects the nature of sociopathy with novelistic intensity and driving force, leading us down the trail tangled trail of destruction."

A brilliant electrical engineer wrote the following:

Figure 3 depicts typical wiring divided into four zones. Zone 0 is associated with the meter, meter socket, and service cable. Zone 1 is associated with the loadcenter and the fixed premise wiring. Zone 2 is associated with the wiring between the receptacles and the loads, and Zone 3 is associated with the appliances and other loads. A good arc fault circuit breaker with ground fault protection will mitigate against parallel arcing and series high resistance faults in zones 1 through 4.

The writer blushed when I pointed out that there is no zone 4 for the circuit breaker to protect unless the main text is wrong; the redundant use of "is associated with" isn't necessary; and the use of "four" in the first sentence is not parallel with the use of the numbers themselves everywhere else. We rewrote the paragraph as follows:

Residential wiring is typically divided into four zones (Figure 3):

- 0, the meter, its socket, and service cable;
- 1, the loadcenter and fixed wiring;
- 2, wiring between receptacles and loads; and
- 3, appliances and other loads.

A good arc fault circuit breaker with ground fault protection will help protect against the hazards of parallel arcing and series high-resistance faults in all zones.

If you can't find a dozen or more similar blips every day in your newspaper or business documents, you're not looking very hard, and you need to fine-tune your poop detector. Try it; it's fun and profitable, too.

9. C'MON, GET TO THE POINT

Quit wasting your readers' valuable time—irritating them to no end, as you know—with windy openers and buried gems of insight. But how do you find the point? See "1. You Can't Communicate if You Can't Empathize" for a hint or two, and examine this letter from my power supplier for additional hints:

> As part of our commitment to provide you with quality service, Duquesne Light will be carrying out maintenance on the electrical distribution system in your neighborhood. To complete this necessary maintenance, your service will be interrupted.
>
> Our crews will be working in your area on January 15, 2006. This outage is scheduled from 8:00 pm to midnight. This letter is intended to give you as much notice as possible so that the interruption of service will be as convenient as possible for you.
>
> If you have any questions please call XXXXXX.

Note the noun "maintenance" in the first sentence could easily be a verb, "maintain," and the several disunities are totally unnecessary and give me the feeling that the writer is trying to fill the page rather than tell me what I need to know. And notice that the meaning of the last sentence in the second paragraph is exactly the opposite of what the writer intended. Can the interruption be as convenient as possible?

Now put yourself in my mind, the empathy we talked about in "1. You Can't Communicate if You Can't Empathize." The only points that interest me are the date, time, and duration of the outage, and they are scattered throughout the letter. The remainder of the letter is public relations that I can do without. Wouldn't it have been better to say the following:

> Your electricity will be off on Sunday, January 15, 2006, from 8 P.M. to midnight while we complete necessary maintenance. (Would "maintain the system" be better?)
>
> We are sorry for the temporary inconvenience.
>
> For further information, please call XXXXX

Too curt and a bit unfriendly? Maybe so—I cut the number of words from 90 to 33, almost by two-thirds, by cutting the PR that I recognize as BS. But on the plus side, I know, quickly and clearly, how and when I will be affected, which is the purpose of the letter.

The following memo was written by the president of a large manufacturer with annual sales over $2 billion and some 2300 employees, all at a campuslike office complex. The purpose of the memo was to ask some employees not to use certain parking lots and cafeterias while visitors attended a conference.

Subject: Meeting on Management by Objective, January 15–17

On January 15–17 the corporation will host a conference on Management by Objective which will be held in Building 6 auditorium.

Approximately 300 conference participants are expected, which will cause crowding at some of the corporation's facilities. The Building 6 parking lot will be reserved for conference attendees. Employees who normally park there should make an effort to use other lots. Also, between 11:30 a.m. and 12:30 p.m., the Administration Building cafeteria will be occupied by conference attendees. Corporation employees should plan accordingly.

As always, your cooperation in these matters is greatly appreciated.

The point—to use other parking lots and cafeterias—is buried in the latter part of the second paragraph, and all employees, even those who do not use the relevant parking lot and cafeteria, must wade through the memo to find out if it applies to them. The memo might read like this if it were more pointed:

Subject: Parking and eating restrictions on January 15–17.

Please do not use the Building 6 parking lot or Administration Building cafeteria during the subject dates. The corporation is hosting some 300 attendees to a conference on Management by Objective, and they will be using those facilities.

As always, thank you for your cooperation.

10. BE PARALLEL WHENEVER POSSIBLE

Parallel construction is a great way to bring order out of chaos. Parallelism is nothing more than using similar grammatical constructions in successive units, whether they are words, phrases, clauses, sentences, paragraphs, numbers, or entire documents. Parallelism is usually thought of as it applies to sentences:

> Americans tend to be optimistic, enthusiastic, and they eat well.

"Optimistic" and "enthusiastic" are adjectives that describe Americans; "they eat well" is an independent clause that describes how Americans live. To be parallel, change to all adjectives, as follows:

> Americans tend to be optimistic, enthusiastic, and well fed.

Another example:

> Pete bought the new car because it is reliable and good on gas.

Change to:

> Pete bought the new car because it is reliable and efficient.

Parallel problems are endemic and more complex than these simple sentences. For example, this sentence from *Harper's* magazine rattled my eyes and ears: "Previous studies have suggested that men with longer ring fingers are more fertile and that women are more fertile if their index fingers are long." This sentence in parallel construction would be considerably shorter and read like this: "Previous studies have suggested that men with longer ring fingers and women with long index fingers are more fertile." Would "longer" instead of "long" index fingers make more sense, and would it be more parallel? Or would it change the meaning?

Not all strings of words or thoughts can be parallel. A local restaurant displays this sign: "We serve lunch, dinner, and catering." Obviously, it can't serve catering, which is an entirely different thought that needs its own clause or phrase, so try this: "We serve lunch and dinner, and cater your private events."

11. START EARLY ON EVERY COMMUNICATIONS ASSIGNMENT

No matter how trivial it may seem, starting early on communications assignments gives your subconscious mind the time needed to do the hard work: fill in the knowledge gaps that the disciplines of writing invariably uncover, and come up with new approaches to communicating that will command attention, which we call "creativity." I'm fond of demonstrating this concept via this statistic: I can write a 20-minute speech that I'm willing to put my name on in about 22 hours, but I need four weeks to put in those hours. I need the downtime to cook my ideas. The operative words are "willing to put my name on." Like you, I can write a 20-minute speech in an hour or two, but I know it will be shallow and incoherent—a bad product that will cost me later in lost business.

The bottom line is, simply, that starting early allows you to produce a better product in fewer hours. That's higher productivity and quality wrapped into one simple habit.

YOU GET TO "ARTICULATE" THE SAME WAY YOU GET TO CARNEGIE HALL

Practice, practice, practice! You hold in your hands at this moment everything you need to start: statistical/scientific and anecdotal evidence that words are, without doubt, your path to success in all parts of life, no matter how it is measured; role models of successful practitioners who have openly and honestly discussed how and why articulation has enhanced their careers and lives; five simple habits called CLOWT, which are the foundation for your clout in the world; and the Elite Eleven Tools that will, I guarantee you, improve your writing and speaking in significant, noticeable ways.

It's all you need to start, except . . .

Your belief and commitment.

Go for it.

PART V

EPILOGUE: IS WHAT'S GOOD FOR THE PERSON GOOD FOR THE GROUP?

*A modest proposal to extend the
benefits of articulation.*

15 Spreading the Word about Words

Organizations of any type and size can reap the benefits of articulation.

T his book focuses on individuals and how they can enrich their lives in many ways via their words. The sequence toward enrichment is clear:

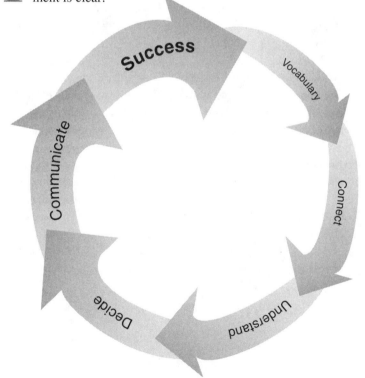

Why should this sequence apply only to individuals? Why not entire families and other organizations? Doesn't it follow with great plausibility, if not certitude, that an organization populated by Articulates would make a greater number (a higher percentage) of informed, logical, and creative decisions than one populated by Also-Rans? And wouldn't that organization enjoy a strong competitive advantage? Isn't articulation a powerful economic and social force?

The individuals profiled in this book recognize these connections by hiring and promoting the most articulate person possible at each level in the organization. They also tend to break the stifling bonds of bureaucracy and create a culture of open, honest communication—a prerequisite for creativity, productivity, and other desirable traits of individuals and organizations. However, they, and I daresay all managers, can go further in several ways that, admittedly, are modest and hesitant first steps toward developing a culture that encourages articulation.

> **If** you as a manager believe that hiring the most articulate person available at any level is in the best interests of your organization . . .
>
> **Then** include in your hiring criteria formal evaluations of each candidate's vocabulary (simple and quantifiable) and abilities to write and speak (more complex and subjective). Joe D, in Chapter 8, tests the writing skills of applicants by evaluating a sample of their best writing; if Joe can't extract a clear meaning after one careful reading, he will likely look for a better candidate. Jim Browne, in Chapter 5, rejects applicants who interrupt other people as they speak or who complete other people's sentences.
>
> **If** you believe that people who are more proficient with language also tend to be more proficient in their regular disciplines . . .
>
> **Then** teach language skills as part of every training program regardless of the topic, which requires some reshuffling of the training curriculum. And require that new hires attend classes in writing and speaking offered by the training department, a local university, or an outside consultant. Offer the classes to veteran employees as well.

If you are convinced that vocabulary is key to articulation . . .

Then offer free of charge any of the many vocabulary-building programs and explain to employees why it's important to subscribe to them. Start crossword contests within the organization that anyone can enter and win significant prizes (perhaps a beat-the-boss crossword contest?).

If you're in the training department or in public/private education at any level . . .

Then recognize that proficiency in the language should be taught before proficiency in the so-called main disciplines, and adjust your curricula accordingly. Read *The One Thing You Cannot Hide*, an audiocassette transcription by Earl Nightingale, and *Ideas Have Consequences*, by Richard Weaver.

One penultimate thought: if articulate individuals and organizations are more powerful economic forces than their also-ran brethren, then why can't families, cities, metropolitan areas, states, and countries harness the same force? Before you dismiss that thought as far-fetched, consider that the root cause of dysfunctional and broken families is, according to many counselors, a breakdown in communications. It follows that the same is true of many businesses and their parts. Consider also that Silicon Valley, Boston, and Seattle, for example, are among the leaders in so-called technological creativity; New York leads in finance; and tiny Santa Fe is among the world's leaders in the visual arts. The United States, by investing 40 percent of the world's total research and development dollars, is the leader in innovation and new-product introductions. Surely other areas and countries can lead in articulation.

Perhaps this is the ultimate thought: if we are living in the information age, then articulate individuals, families, organizations, and countries will rule the world.

Peter Drucker noted years ago that the basic economic resources, the means of production, are no longer capital, labor, or natural resources; the means are wrapped in that broad term "knowledge." As we've already seen, knowledge is useless without the means to transmit it, which is the job of information technology, and to explain and apply it—the job of the Articulates.

Bibliography

Relevant Studies

Gershon, R. C. *The Vocabulary Scores of Managers*. Technical Report 1990-5. Chicago: Johnson O'Connor Research Foundation, 1990.

Smith, R. M., and G. Supanich. *The Vocabulary Scores of Company Presidents*. Technical Report 1984-1. Chicago: Johnson O'Connor Research Foundation, 1984.

A Study of the English Vocabulary Scores of Company Presidents. Technical Report 2. Boston: Human Engineering Laboratory, 1935.

Supanich, G., and B. Ingram. *Analysis and Revision of Vocabulary Worksample 708*. Technical Report 1985-4. Chicago: Johnson O'Connor Research Foundation, 1985.

Books about Words and Their Uses

Bryson, Bill. *Bryson's Dictionary of Troublesome Words*. New York: Broadway Books, 2002.

Lovinger, Paul W. *The Penguin Dictionary of American English Usage and Style*. New York: Penguin Reference, 2000.

Merriam-Webster's Concise Handbook for Writers. Springfield, MA: Merriam-Webster, 1998.

Safire, William. *The Right Word in the Right Place at the Right Time*. New York: Simon & Schuster, 2004.

Books about Writing and Thinking

Horton, Susan R. *Thinking through Writing*. Baltimore: Johns Hopkins University Press, 1982.

Leary, William G., and James Steel Smith. *Think before You Write*. New York: Harcourt Brace and Company, 1951.

Weaver, Richard M. *Ideas Have Consequences*. Chicago: University of Chicago Press, 1948.

Zinsser, William. *Writing to Learn*. New York: Harper and Row, 1988.

Writing/Communicating on the Job

Campanizzi, Jane. *Effective Writing for the Quality Professional: Creating Useful Letters, Reports, and Procedures*. Milwaukee: ASQ Quality Press, 2005.

Dragga, Sam, Kenneth W. Houp, Thomas E. Pearsall, and Elizabeth Tebeaux. *Reporting Technical Information*. 11th ed. New York: Oxford University Press, 2005.

Hoffman, Gary, and Glynis Hoffman. *Adios, Strunk and White*. 2nd ed. Huntington Beach, CA: Verve Press, 1999.

Kolin, Philip C. *Successful Writing at Work*. 7th ed. Boston: Houghton Mifflin, 2004.

Lannon, John M. *Technical Writing*. Glenview, IL: Scott, Foresman and Company, 1988.

Marshall, Lisa J., and Lucy D. Freedman. *Smart Work*. Dubuque, IA: Kendall/Hunt, 1995.

Pfeiffer, William S. *Technical Writing: A Practical Approach*. 2nd ed. New York: Merrill, 1994.

Williams, Joseph M. *Style: Toward Clarity and Grace*. Chicago: University of Chicago Press, 1990.

Quips about Writing and Writers

Peter, Laurence J. *Peter's Quotations: Ideas for our Time*. New York: Morrow, 1977.

Winokur, Jon. *W.O.W. Writers on Writing*. Philadelphia: Running Press, 1990.

Index

Bucenell, Rob, 56
bulleted lists, 109–110
Bush, George W., 52, 75
business, as metaphysical
   community, 8
business meetings, 54–55

C
Chaplin, Charlie, 7
chunking, 109–110, 114
clients
   emotional quotient of, 42–45
   kid-glove approach to, 46–47
Clinton, Bill, 76–77
CLOWT (compartmentalize, listen,
   organize, write, test), 21–25,
   76–77, 98, 99
cohesion, 110–112
colons, 115–116
commas, uses of, 115–116
communication
   computers and, 12–13
   defined, 8
   managers and, 9–10
   persuasion as goal of, 25
compartmentalizing, 22
computers, communication and,
   12–13
Cosby, Bill, 16
cultural change, articulation and,
   37–38

D
dash, 115–116
Didion, Joan, 14
Douglas, Stephen A., 9
Drucker, Peter, 10, 127

E
Elite Eleven Tools, 98, 99, 107–121.
   See also writing
   ABC structure, 112–114

active voice, 114–115
allowing adequate time, 121
avoiding miscues, 116–117
being succinct, 118–119
cohesion, 110–112
lists, 109–110
parallelism, 120–121
proper use of dash, comma,
   semicolon, and colon,
   115–116
reader profiles, 107–109
verbs from nouns, 115
Emerson, Ralph Waldo, 6
emotional quotient (EQ), of clients,
   42–45
empathy, with audiences,
   107–109
environmental business/profession,
   writing and, 12
Eshleman, Russell E., Jr., 9

G
GenCorp, 35–40
Gordimer, Nadine, 23
Gore, Al, 52, 75
Green, Dave, 51
Guth, Sherry Davis, 57–61

H
Hawking, Stephen, 9–10
Hemingway, Ernest, 116–117
Hockenbury, Don H., 14
Hockenbury, Sandra E., 14
Homer, 7
Hutchinson, Earl Ofari, 16

I
Iacocca, Lee, 24
inarticulation. *See also* articulation
   business meetings and, 54–55
   example of, 87–89
   high cost of, 81–87

T

TelCove, 57–61

tracking, 110–112

V

verbs, making nouns from, 115

vocabulary

building, 103–104

as foundation of articulation,
13–14

hiring Articulates and,
126–127

of managers, *vs.* presidents, 15

success and, 15–16

W

Weaver, Richard, 8, 10, 17, 127

Wilkinson, Monte, 54

writing, 11–12. *See also* Elite
Eleven Tools

Articulates and, 23–24

environmental business/
profession and, 12

paths to good, 98–99

succinctness in, 118–119

Y

Yasinsky, John, 18, 25, 29–30, 51

alignment and, 38

on articulation, 38–39

articulation as key to success for,
38–39

early years of, 30

as head of GenCorp, 35–40

lessons learned by, 39–40

set of Behavioral Expectations
of, 37–38

at Westinghouse, 33–34

as White House Fellow, 30–33

Z

Zinsser, William, 24